WHAT IT TAKES

WHAT IT TAKES

SARINA WIEGMAN

WITH JEROEN VISSCHER

MY PLAYBOOK ON LIFE
AND LEADERSHIP

HarperCollins*Publishers*

HarperCollins*Publishers*
1 London Bridge Street
London SE1 9GF

www.harpercollins.co.uk

HarperCollins*Publishers*
Macken House, 39/40 Mayor Street Upper
Dublin 1, D01 C9W8, Ireland

First published by HarperCollins*Publishers* 2023

10 9 8 7 6 5 4 3 2 1

© Sarina Wiegman and Jeroen Visscher 2023

Translated by Andrew Davies, Chapter & Verse
www.chapterandverse.nl

Sarina Wiegman asserts the moral right to
be identified as the author of this work

A catalogue record of this book is
available from the British Library

HB ISBN 978-0-00-864804-6
PB ISBN 978-0-008-67296-6

Printed and bound in the UK using 100%
renewable electricity at CPI Group (UK) Ltd

MIX
Paper | Supporting
responsible forestry
FSC
www.fsc.org FSC™ C007454

This book contains FSC™ certified paper and other controlled
sources to ensure responsible forest management.

For more information visit: www.harpercollins.co.uk/green

For my parents Toon and Bep(†), my twin brother Tom and my sister Diana(†), my husband Marten, and my daughters Sacha and Lauren

CONTENTS

PART TWO
A NEW GENERATION

PROLOGUE

**Sunday 16 July, opening game of Euro 2017
in the Netherlands**

THE NETHERLANDS VS NORWAY

As soon as I open my eyes, I know the day I've been waiting for has finally come. At precisely six o'clock in the evening we're scheduled to kick off the opening game of Euro 2017 against Norway and the Galgenwaard stadium in Utrecht will be filled to the rafters. This day marks the beginning of our journey towards fulfilling our ultimate dream. Our primary objective is to play our best football for our supporters.

When I rise from bed, the significance of the occasion strikes me with full force. Memories of my own days playing football as a young girl come flooding back to me. I remember the time when I first started playing the sport at the age of six. Back then, women's football had only just been acknowledged by the KNVB, the Royal Dutch Football Association. However, even as a young girl, it was still impossible to join a club. Undeterred, I boldly cut off my hair and joined anyway. Despite the fact that it was technically illegal, my parents always let me play football. And now, as I stand on the cusp of a new chapter in my footballing journey, the Dutch women's national football team – universally known as the Leeuwinnen* – are poised to play in the Euros to a capacity crowd on home soil.

The magnitude of the moment isn't lost on me, and I can't help but feel a sense of pride and gratitude for the path that has led me to this point.

It makes me happy, prompting me to reach out to my father with a message of heartfelt gratitude. I express my appreciation for the fact that we're both alive to witness this day and share with him just how fantastic it feels to be a part of it all. As I type out the words, a surge of emotion overtakes me. It's something truly special. The sheer excitement is simply indescribable. Indeed, this is just the beginning – a thrilling new chapter in my life that promises to be nothing short of extraordinary.

---

* It's a great irony that the Dutch word *Leeuwinnen* means 'Lionesses', given that I was later to coach another team with that name.

As we board the coach for the brief journey from our training camp in Zeist, the atmosphere is palpable, full of anticipation for the upcoming match at Galgenwaard. Observing the team, I'm struck by their unwavering focus, each player with their own unique approach to achieving optimal concentration.

The concept of 'focus' is set to play a critical role this day. Several months earlier I sought the expertise of an eye specialist as I was starting to have difficulty reading. Because of my aversion to glasses I opted to try contact lenses, despite the specialist's warning that my eyes are too sensitive to wear them. As might be expected, the specialist's prediction proves accurate, but I find myself grappling with the question of how far I'm willing to go to avoid wearing glasses. Will I be able to reconcile this dilemma on the day of the match?

The road from Zeist to the stadium is badly congested, and I can make out a long line of cars stretching into the distance. I can't help but wonder why everyone has to be on the road at that moment. Suddenly it hits me. They're all heading to the stadium car park to catch the shuttle buses that will take them the short distance to the game. They're on their way to cheer us on!

As we take the Galgenwaard exit and make a left turn towards the stadium, a wave of excitement washes over me. The sight of thousands of spirited Dutch fans congregating on the stadium concourse, eagerly anticipating our performance, gives me goosebumps. The euphoria that surges through my body is indescribable. It's a momentous day for women's football in the Netherlands, and I feel privileged to be a part of it. When I survey my surroundings, I realise that I'm not the only one moved by the scenes outside. Tears are welling in the eyes of the players and coaching staff. This remarkable and emotional moment will go down in football history. Today's the day we've been waiting for!

Amid the throngs of people I spot my husband Marten. It's an uncanny coincidence that, out of the thousands of people present, he's the one I notice first. It feel as if fate is telling me something.

As soon as we enter the stadium we receive some surprising news about the Norway line-up. Whenever we assess our opponents, we consider all the different starting options they might use. In this case, Norway have made some changes to their usual line-up and have adapted to our system. It's definitely a surprise, but we've prepared for it and are ready to face the challenge.

The tears I've shed at the emotion of the occasion have dried up, but as the warm-up begins I start to have trouble with my contact lenses. Despite having them in, I find it impossible to focus, so I rush inside to remove them.

Thankfully, my eyes adjust quickly and I'm able to return to the pitch in no time.

We've put a lot of effort into planning for these games, but there's always an element of uncertainty. Just 17 seconds after the referee blows her whistle to start the game, Jackie Groenen threads a precise ball through to Shanice van de Sanden out on the right. She crosses to Lieke Martens on the far side, who manages to get past her defender and take a shot at goal. It's a close call but doesn't quite squeeze in, the Norwegian keeper making a reflex save to her left. We don't let it get us down, though, confident that things will work out in the end.

INTRODUCTION

It's 20 July 2022 and we're in the midst of the England vs Spain match at Euro 2022. I shift my gaze to the right, where Arjan Veurink – the former assistant coach of the Leeuwinnen and now assistant coach of the Lionesses team – sits. I notice a hint of curiosity in his expression. A quick nod is enough to convey our understanding. We know exactly what we have to do. With just eight minutes left on the clock, the Lionesses find themselves one goal behind in the quarter-final against Spain.

We'd practised this precise situation earlier that year during the Arnold Clark Cup, an invitational international competition. Whenever we were behind against a tough opponent we'd immediately switch to Plan B to try and score an equaliser. So now we bring on Alex Greenwood for Rachel Daly and shift Millie Bright higher up the pitch. For me to be able to make that nod is a small miracle in itself. Only at three o'clock this afternoon, six hours prior to the match, did I receive a fully-negative Covid-19 test result. Managing the past few days has been challenging, as we strive to minimize the impact of the virus. Though I felt fine, I had to isolate myself for several days. As a result, I wasn't able to coach the match against Northern Ireland in person. All team discussions were conducted outside, with me wearing a face mask to maintain a healthy distance from everyone else. I am deeply concerned about the possibility of infecting players, and I don't even want to entertain the thought of that happening.

Knowing that Covid-19 could impact on the Euros, and with the regular visits I made to see my gravely ill sister in the Netherlands during the lead-up to the tournament, we found ourselves forced to prepare for the possibility of my absence during a match. Our team hotel had now been set up so that I could coach the quarter-final against Spain from there, and on the morning of the match I'd already taken a test. So the doctor suggested I test again as late as possible before the match kicks off at 8 pm, and I spent the afternoon walking and doing relaxation exercises to mentally prepare myself for the results, starting to doubt myself more and more. But then comes the doctor's reassuring news. My test is negative, and I'm cleared to go to the stadium. This outcome immediately gives a boost to the team. In fact, we were already 1–0 ahead.

And so I'm now standing in the stadium. The nod, the substitution, Plan B. Less than two minutes later, the cross from the right is skilfully headed down by Alessia Russo and the incoming Ella Toone ruthlessly strikes it into the net. The joy, the relief, the conviction that we're now going to win: a year of working with this team culminates in this single moment.

But there's little time for celebration as the score is still only level at 1–1 and we're not yet through to the semi-final. On the pitch I can see that the players are executing our plan. We know that Plan B is only meant to secure an equaliser and that playing like that for an extended period against a strong opponent like Spain would be naive. So Millie Bright shifts back to defence and we return to Plan A, knowing that there's drama yet to come. Spain have been mentally affected by our equaliser and are starting to falter, while the determination within our team is evident. Moreover, we appear fitter and fresher, and we can make use of that in extra-time.

In the 96th minute I can see it all unfolding before my eyes. We've maintained our pressure on Spain, and after they lose the ball, Georgia Stanway receives a crucial pass in midfield. She surges forward unchallenged, and after an extra touch that deceives the goalkeeper, unleashes a powerful shot that bulges the left side of the net. It's a moment of huge release as the score shifts to 2–1 in our favour.

Jorge Vilda, the Spanish national coach, now reacts swiftly by pushing Irene Paredes up from central defence, but I can sense her uncertainty in her new role. Spain are becoming sloppier and we gain more control of the game.

Pure joy fills the air when the referee blows the final whistle. I immediately look for Arjan and the rest of the staff so that we can celebrate together. This match holds immense significance for us, and winning it means the world to the team. Throughout the match I couldn't stop myself from wondering, *What if we lose to Spain?* We'd played exceptionally well thus far in the tournament, and a loss would have undermined all that we'd previously achieved. But that worry has been put to rest. We're now brimful of confidence heading into our semi-final against Sweden, knowing that we've got what it takes to come out on top. We feel that we're engaged in something really special.

This moment was one of the many defining moments in my coaching career in women's football. It was important because it made us realise that we had a fantastic opportunity to fulfil our dreams. It wasn't just our tactical intervention that turned the match around. As a team, we now knew we had the resilience to recover from a setback

– going behind to Spain's goal – and turn things in our favour. Apart from progressing to the next stage of the competition, the feeling of confidence and belief that this victory instilled was the most valuable outcome of the quarter-final.

Throughout my career I've experienced numerous critical moments, both positive and negative, that have shaped me as a coach. The value of these cannot be overstated in such a demanding profession as football coaching. I've always been open to learning from feedback and engaging in self-reflection, and I'm fortunate to be surrounded by professionals who share the same desire as me: to improve and grow daily with the team. Embracing feedback and using it as a tool for learning is something we do collectively as both staff and players, regardless of our diverse backgrounds and cultures. It demands a lot, but it's crucial for our development.

Football has been my passion since I was a young girl. The love I have for the game has always been a driving force for me, even during times when expressing that love was challenging. I remember the disapproval I had to face for being a girl playing a supposedly boys' game, and cutting my hair short as a young player so I wouldn't stand out as much on the boys' team I played for. As a rookie coach I had to work tirelessly to pursue my ambitions and make ends meet financially.

I can't quite fathom how I managed, but during that period I'd just qualified as a PE teacher and combined my own football career with following the UEFA A coaching programme at the Central Institution for the Education of Sports Leaders (CIOS), studying on Sundays and working at the KNVB to pay for my studies. That's only possible if you can fall back on your family, and happily for me that was possible. For my parents, our family, my husband Marten and our daughters there was no doubt. They supported me so that I could do what I liked doing.

What It Takes: My Playbook on Life and Leadership delves deep into my passions: football, and working with ambitious and talented people. This is where my heart lies. Football provides me with an incredible amount of energy, and it's important for me to give something back to football. People often describe what I do as remarkable, but when I reflect on my journey I don't find it extraordinary. This is simply who I am, and I find immense joy in what others might consider challenging.

Certainly, being the England women's national team coach demands a lot from me. There are no days off when you have this responsibility. Even when I had Covid-19 during Euro 2022, I felt the pressure to return as soon as possible, despite that, of course, not being possible. Similarly, when my sister Diana passed away just before the tournament began, the Football Association gave me some leeway, but I couldn't escape the fact that all eyes were on me as the national team coach. I'm always in the spotlight, and that can be tough at times. In those moments, I long to be able to switch off and just be with my family.

I found it particularly challenging during the weeks before Diana's passing. During the latter stages of her life and the week following her death, including her cremation, all the focus was on Diana, and I stepped away from football.

To me, football is all about the game, the development and being part of a team. It's an incredibly captivating sport: the playful element, the beauty of it when executed to perfection and the exhilaration of winning a match.

One particular moment stands out as an epitome of perfection, the goal against Brazil in the first ever Women's Finalissima in 2023. It was a moment of flawless teamwork, starting with a phenomenal attack initiated from our defence, a precise pass out to our right side and an orchestrated collaboration involving multiple players. The ball was eventually laid back to Ella Toone by Lucy Bronze, and Ella powerfully swept it into the corner. As a coach I relish these moments from the dug-out. It's the style of play that we aspire to, and witnessing the connection between players fills me with an indescribable sense of satisfaction. At that point, I literally feel my passion.

Development is a vital aspect of my passion, one that extends beyond the boundaries of football. The growth of the team, the players, the staff and myself are of utmost importance. Without this element, I wouldn't be a coach. Facilitating the growth of individuals has been a constant source of joy throughout my life, whether as a player, a PE teacher or now as a coach. It's incredibly fulfilling to provide opportunities for players to develop and thrive at the highest level, and within our environment their personal growth is directly correlated to their performance. Elite athletes demand so much of themselves to deliver top-notch performances that a supportive and accepting atmosphere is essential.

For me, passion is also synonymous with the team. I rarely use the word 'I' because it is always about the collective. This applies to both the players and the staff. Achieving excellence means developing and improving individuals, but the ultimate goal is to strengthen the team as a whole. When a player flourishes in her role within the team, we become a stronger unit. And when we can showcase our strength through victories, we become the best together. This is the essence of my passion.

I feel a responsibility to share my love for football and in so doing, above all, inspire girls and women to make football their career, in whatever role. As a coach, I've been fortunate to make a positive impact with my teams.

And, first and foremost, we must continue doing this, because there's still a long way to go.

Things have definitely improved since I was obliged to play football with boys when I was younger, but there's still a long way to go. Things are moving forward, but equal opportunities have still not been achieved. I hope that my book can help change that. Every woman who wants to play or coach football should have the chance to show her talent. I understand how important it is for young girls and women to have role models and feel confident, and I hope my experiences can pave the way for their growth.

My dream is to see equal opportunities for everyone in the sport I adore. Together, we can inspire the next generation to see the beauty of football. When young girls proudly wear the jerseys of players like Millie Bright, Lauren James, Mary Earps, Lieke Martens, Vivianne Miedema or Esmee Brugts, they'll know that they too can dream of appearing in a final someday.

Throughout my coaching journey I've had the privilege of working with top professionals. In elite sports it's crucial to surround yourself with the best players and staff. Without them I wouldn't have achieved what I have, and it's important to me that they're part of my story too.

I share my story through the pivotal moments that I've been a part of. It could be during the intense preparation for a tournament, a significant match or a memorable experience in my coaching career. Every moment, big or small, matters. The details need to come together for success.

PART ONE

KEY MILESTONES ON MY FOOTBALL JOURNEY

1

LAYING THE GROUNDWORK FOR SUCCESS

IS THIS WHAT YOU WANT TO DO?

I heard Hans van Breukelen, who was the technical director of the KNVB at that time, ask the question: 'Are you prepared to take on the role of the national team coach?' As it happened, I'd been asked this same question twice before, and on both occasions I'd requested a bit of time in which to reflect before giving an answer. The world of football is still a male-dominated space, so it's not surprising that as a woman I was asked whether I was ready and willing to step up to become coach of the Dutch national women's team, the Leeuwinnen.

In my opinion, it's crucial to provide a carefully considered response to such a question, especially when it presents significant new opportunities. But rather than answering straight away, it's important to take the question home and discuss it with your partner and children, your family and friends. The impact of your decision will often be far-reaching, so it's essential to consider the perspectives of those closest to you.

The likelihood is high, even in today's society, that a man will interpret things differently than a woman. I myself have experienced this very situation. When I gave my response, I felt doubt arise from across the table, although I'd intended the opposite. My aim was to provide assurance, by carefully considering my answer.

Having previously been in a similar situation, I learned to adapt when in the presence of male decision-makers. So this time, I responded confidently that I was ready. I felt it, and I had the impression that they did too.

MY DEBUT AS NATIONAL TEAM COACH

As a coach I've been lucky enough to work with talented and committed people who've played a role in shaping my career. One moment that stands out is when I was chosen to be the coach of the Leeuwinnen, the Dutch women's national football team. I still remember the encouraging words of Jan Dirk van der Zee of the KNVB. He expressed his faith in my abilities and my football philosophy. It was a big step both for me and for the

KNVB, and in just a few months we started a movement in the Netherlands that couldn't be stopped.

Jan Dirk van der Zee, director of the Koninklijke Nederlandse Voetbalbond (KNVB)

After Arjan van der Laan's spell as manager of the Leeuwinnen from October 2015 to December 2016, we were presented with some stark truths and learned some valuable lessons. If you have no experience of or affinity with the women's game, the chances of becoming a success-ful trainer aren't great.

Hans van Breukelen was appointed as technical director to further develop both men's and women's football in the Netherlands. At a meeting to discuss candidates for the position of manager following Van der Laan's departure, it wasn't long before we focused on Sarina Wiegman. She met our most essential criteria: a distinguished international football playing career, prior managerial experience at club level and possession of a UEFA Pro coaching licence. She had also served as an assistant to Van der Laan.

During her tenure as assistant coach, however, it appeared that Sarina could also be quite difficult to work with. She hadn't established much rapport with Van der Laan and was already asserting her authority inside the dressing room. She set high standards for the coaching team, and if any team members fell short of these she made her feelings abundantly clear.

Could we dare appoint her in the run-up to such a significant tournament as Euro 2017? Well, we took a chance. We discussed it with her, with Hans asking the questions, and Sarina's passion left a powerful impression on me. How had her incredible vision escaped my attention until this point and how had we made such a grave error at an earlier stage? It was now time to put things right.

Our discussions yielded the desired outcome. Sarina became the new head coach of the Leeuwinnen. From then on, she had the opportunity to put her vision into practice with the team, even though time was limited. In collaboration with Sarina, we assembled a coaching team that measured up to her stringent requirements. Arjan Veurink was the coach of the women's team at FC Twente, and we recognised him as a promising talent. Sarina also understood the importance of recruiting experienced staff members, and that's how we ended up connecting with Foppe de Haan, the former coach of teams like SC Heerenveen, Jong Oranje (Young Netherlands) and Ajax Cape Town. When he agreed to join us, the foundation for our new technical staff was set.

BUILDING TEAMS: CREATING CERTAINTY AMONG THE STAFF, 2017

I became the coach of the Dutch national women's team back in January 2017, an intense experience right from the beginning as within just a few weeks we had to get things organised that normally take several months. However, because much of the preparation for the 2017 European Championship was already done – and I knew the coaching staff and players well – we were able to accomplish it. The main challenge was assembling a complete coaching staff while at the same time working closely with the team. I also wanted to make sure that the selection and coaching staff got off to a good start, which demanded a lot from me. It highlighted how much I relied on the support of my family, as I was away from home a lot.

The first order of business in our planning for Euro 2017 was to host a staff meeting. Since I was working with a sizeable group of approximately 20 people, the primary objective of the meeting was to clarify the nature of everyone's respective roles. While staff members could take on additional responsibilities, it was essential that their tasks and duties were well defined from the outset so that everyone was aware of what was expected of them every step of the way. This approach helped to enhance transparency and motivate the staff to set a positive example for the players. It was critical for staff members to be supportive, constructive and encouraging with the players, thereby creating a conducive environment for learning and development.

At that time, Arjan Veurink and Foppe de Haan had not yet been chosen as assistant coaches. I was in ongoing discussions with Arjan to figure out the specific details of his role, while Foppe was serving as a consultant for the Leeuwinnen. As far as I was concerned, this latter arrangement was not working. While I was having discussions with my coaching staff, I also had to have the same conversations with Foppe, as his consultant role didn't provide much value and felt rather pointless. Foppe needed to be fully committed to our team – or not at all.

I had a discussion with Foppe about this, which was not altogether straightforward for me because he was an accomplished and highly respected coach. He'd always been a head coach, someone who took charge, called the shots, provided a clear vision, and he was very vocal with the media. I, on the other hand, was more reserved, and although I was the new head coach of the Leeuwinnen, people didn't yet know what to expect from me. But I knew exactly how I wanted things to be.

It was essential to have an unambiguous hierarchy, with one head coach in overall control, so I had to establish clear boundaries and areas of responsibility with Foppe to prevent things from spiralling into chaos. This clarity was crucial for the players, as well as for public relations. We had detailed discussions to outline the nature of our collaboration, highlighting my specific expectations for Foppe. While he found much of this challenging to accept, he also recognised it was the only way to proceed. We both appreciated the openness and honesty of these discussions, even though I hadn't really been looking forward to them. However, I sensed that that they were absolutely crucial to our successful collaboration, and I was amazed how such an esteemed coach like Foppe was able to adapt to this new situation.

This marked the beginning of a fruitful and valued partnership, although there were moments of breakdown along the way. During Euro 2017, for instance, Foppe expressed his enthusiasm about one of our players to the media shortly before a game. When I discovered this later that evening, I knew I had to address the matter promptly. The following morning I spoke with Foppe to remind him that this was not what we had agreed upon. While it may have made him uncomfortable, I felt it was necessary to take this action. Foppe acknowledged and respected my decision, understanding the importance of sticking to our agreements, and he no longer engaged in any media activities.

This was a significant milestone in my journey as a head coach. I made sure to issue clear instructions not only to my junior staff, but also to the senior assistants. Whenever they deviated too far from what we had agreed upon, it created tension. However, once I addressed the situation, I could sense their appreciation for the open and respectful manner in which I handled it.

Throughout my coaching career I've learned a great deal from my fellow coaches. One person I've always held in high regard is Louis van Gaal, known for his expertise and passion for coaching. To me, he's a true visionary and pioneer in our field. During our conversations I always discovered something new, and I soon realised that we have more in common than meets the eye.

Louis van Gaal, former head coach of the Netherlands men's team

The first time I met Sarina was at her 100th international match as a player for the Leeuwinen. I was the head coach of the Dutch men's team, and I spoke at the game at the KNVB's request. Playing so many international matches is impressive, and I knew Sarina was about to retire as a player. During her celebration I brought up the possibility of her becoming a successful coach since she already met several requirements.

First, Sarina had a lot of experience as a player. She played in midfield and defence, positions that require a good awareness of the spaces around you. In my opinion, possessing this awareness is fundamental to becoming a good coach. Second, Sarina went through the Academy of Physical Education and worked as a PE teacher. Famous figures such as Rinus Michels, Guus Hiddink and Leo Beenhakker have shown that this combination often produces successful coaches. Of course, success isn't guaranteed, but Sarina had the essential ingredients.

Soon after, Arjan Veurink joined the team as an assistant coach. I knew Arjan from our previous matches as opponents, when he was the head coach for FC Twente and I was steering the ship at ADO Den Haag. Knowing that he too had experience in the top role, I wanted to ensure it wouldn't create any little niggles in our collaboration, and as it turned out it didn't. In fact, Arjan found the challenge of working with me and the Leeuwinnen – and accomplishing remarkable feats with us – so compelling that he accepted a non-head coach position. We were both content with this change, and Arjan transitioned from being the main man in the spotlight to assuming a supporting but still vital role.

The central point that we hammered out in our discussion was defining a set of tasks and duties that would enable him to excel. He possessed strong tactical abilities, excelled in providing guidance during training sessions and took responsibility for his actions, and during the years that we worked together we both grew tremendously in our respective positions. My confidence in his abilities meant I could loosen the reins and give him more freedom. This kind of collaboration requires mutual respect and trust, and it took some time for me to feel comfortable delegating certain tasks to other members of staff. But as my confidence in my colleagues grew, I became more relaxed and granted them their own responsibilities.

Foppe, Arjan and I shared several crucial qualities that fostered effective teamwork. We were all deeply invested in understanding the behaviour of the players both on and off the pitch. We wanted to discover what motivated them and how we could use this knowledge to create a stronger, more cohesive team.

After Arjan joined the team, I wanted to make better use of Foppe's expertise. To begin with, Foppe sat next to me on the bench during games, but given his more than 40 years of experience as a coach, it wasn't easy for him to relinquish control completely to me, so we made some changes to the way we worked together and focused on his strengths. During games he would sit high up in the stands for better game analysis. We would then communicate before half-time so he could give feedback to the players in the dressing room. This arrangement worked exceptionally well. Additionally, Foppe spent time with the players, explaining various in-play strategies using his notes. He was an invaluable sounding board for me because he had such a wealth of coaching experience to draw from, as well as a background in teaching sports sciences, just like me.

Lieke Martens was one of the Leeuwinnen players during Euro 2017, the tournament that really showed the world her true talent and skill. With her creativity on the pitch she quickly became a successful and beloved player for Dutch fans, and thanks to these performances she won the 2016–17 UEFA's Women's Player of the Year Award.

I was able to effectively showcase Lieke's strengths by giving her a free role on the pitch and relieve the pressure on her. The synergy between us worked out well as a result.

Lieke Martens, Leeuwinnen forward

Sarina has an unrivalled understanding of women's football. When she first started she had a clear vision of what needed to be done, worked well with every player and had the advantage of having previously worked closely with us all.

We were looking for a coach who could bring a sense of calm to the team and who would take women's football in the Netherlands to new heights. For me, there was no other candidate. Choosing Sarina was a no-brainer, the obvious choice.

Just before Euro 2017, women's football had been undergoing a remarkable development, albeit not one fully recognised by a wider audience. The fact that the Euros were taking place on home soil made it even more special, although we were seen as one of the underdogs and not expected to achieve much. However, we believed in our potential and were determined to prove everyone wrong. Sarina gave us the freedom to play attacking football and was able to get us to play to our own strengths. She was focused on the development of individual players to serve the interests of the team.

She placed immense trust in me and gave me the freedom to play my game. Sarina always played me on the left in a relatively unrestricted role. I was allowed to make forward runs, be in a position to receive the ball and even contribute to the midfield. The amount of freedom she granted me eased the pressure to perform creatively. When I look back on the tournament, it still gives me a great deal of pleasure.

LEARNING TO EMBRACE RESISTANCE

Once our coaching team was established, we were ready to prepare for Euro 2017, set to take place later that year in the Netherlands. One significant benefit of transitioning from the assistant coach role of the national team to head coach is having familiarity with how the organisation operates and who does what. The planning and preparations up until Euro 2017 had already been worked out. This helped tremendously when it came to picking a squad as I knew this group of players extremely well. I was aware of their potential, as well as knowing their beliefs and doubts, so the staff and I already had a good idea of the make-up of the squad.

Our greatest uncertainty in the final selection was the number of injuries in our defence. Merel van Dongen was working her way back from injury, and we had particular concern about Stefanie van der Gragt – also injured – and whether she'd be able to regain her fitness and be in top shape in time for the Euros. We announced the squad on 14 June, earlier than required – the final squad needed to be submitted to UEFA by 5 July – but we'd learned from previous tournaments that announcing the squad early was essential in calming players' nerves during the lead-up to the tournament. At our final training camp ahead of 14

June we faced some tough decisions, with the nine players who were not selected remaining on standby until 5 July.

The most high-profile player who didn't make the cut was Merel van Dongen, and telling her this was a difficult conversation.

Merel van Dongen, Leeuwinnen defender

I've known Sarina since I was 16. She'd been eager for me to join her at Ter Leede, a satellite club for ADO Den Haag, since it was a short distance away from ADO. My initial impression of her was that she was a competent coach who knew what she was talking about. It was a significant moment for me when Sarina expressed interest in me, even though I declined her offer.

In the end, I did end up making the move to Ter Leede. Sarina's first action was to bench me, a new experience for me because I wasn't used to it. Just before the transfer deadline she brought in Tessel Middag, who was a year older than me and also a midfielder. Such a move is just a normal part of the job in top-level sports, but I didn't see this transfer coming. Sarina had already been working with the team and doing all that was needed for the team to win, and she saw the signing of Tessel as another step on that road to success.

Sarina was as tough as they come. That kind of toughness was necessary for success, so we had to accept it. She was never unpleasant, but good enough simply wasn't good enough. And it always had to be better. Winning was the goal.

I had to put in a lot of hard work. Through my experiences with Sarina, I became a lot tougher mentally. Maybe it wasn't just because of her as a person, but because of the decisions she made. Those decisions, both in Sarina's career and my own, haven't always worked out in my favour. If anything, many of them went against me. Despite that, throughout the many years we've worked together there's always been a mutual respect between us.

For years I've been trying to figure it out. There's something about Sarina that sets her apart. The main reason is that she can be tough when it comes to matters on the pitch, but at the same time soft when it concerns the individual. She was aware of the impact her decisions would have on me. In fact, she supported them. It's tough for any elite athlete to handle being dropped. Throughout my career I've had many coaches who were tough on players. They wouldn't listen when a player needed support. They would be vague or evasive. They would give false hope when there was none.

This is where Sarina truly excels. She may be as tough as they come, but she also knows how to help players recognise their strengths, how to make things easier for each individual. When you're young and decisions don't go your way, you don't understand. It's only later on that you start to grasp the reasoning behind them. The reason I hold her in such high esteem is that we've gone through the highs and lows together along this journey.

As a coach, telling players that they 'haven't' made the team is one of the toughest moments for me. It's heart-wrenching to break the news that their dreams of playing in a major tournament won't be realised. It can happen before or during the tournament, and it's never easy. When it takes place during the home Euros – like it did for Tessel Middag, who was unable to be included due to a knee injury – it's especially difficult. It was also tough to make the decision to substitute Mandy van den Berg midway through the tournament. On 14 June I had to have a conversation with Merel and let her know that she wouldn't be joining the team. This was hard because I knew her well and appreciated how much she wanted to play. It's always a tough pill to swallow for the players – and I found it equally challenging.

Merel van Dongen, Leeuwinnen defender

In 2016 I was playing for the Leeuwinnen and my career was on the up. The team's manager, Arjan van der Laan, had been let go, with Sarina appointed as his replacement. In

January 2017, only six months before the Euros, I suffered a severe injury – a damaged knee cartilage – and I didn't fully recover until the end of April. Despite the chronic pain, I kept it to myself because I was determined to play.

On 4 June we had our final training camp before the tournament began, and I was incredibly nervous about whether or not I'd be selected for the provisional squad. I hadn't played for months and was eager for some match practice. To my great relief I was chosen for the provisional squad, and I believed that this meant a spot was reserved for me in the final squad.

However, the real test came on 14 June, the day when Sarina would reveal the final squad. I'd played in neither of the two friendlies leading up to the final squad announcement, which left me feeling frustrated. I asked Sarina if I could have a chat with her about it, but she said that she'd speak with me the following morning. As I went to bed that night, I was left in a state of uncertainty.

After finishing breakfast, I made my way to an adjacent room for the meeting. As soon as I saw the three chairs, I knew that I wouldn't be joining the team for the Euros. It finally dawned on me that my lack of playing time was not because I'd be chosen for the team, but because I wouldn't.

As the conversation progressed, a sense of anger began to build inside me. I managed to keep my composure, however, and suggested to Sarina and Arjan that we end the conversation before I said anything. Although brief, the interview left me feeling like my world had shattered.

When I returned to my hotel room, which I shared with Loes Geurts and Mandy van den Berg, I told them the news. They had not expected this outcome either. I told them I was going to return home immediately, but they encouraged me to attend the final meeting, where those who'd been chosen for the team would receive information about the upcoming training and preparation for the Euros. Despite their encouragement, all I wanted to do was go home.

Looking back on it now, I realise that I shouldn't have attended that final meeting at all. As a professional, however, I felt obliged to do what the coach had asked of me. I sat at the back of the room with tears streaming down my face, hoping that no one would notice. It took me roughly three months to fully recover from the news. During that time I cried frequently, sharing my anger on a talk show with Beau van Erven Dorens, a well-known Dutch television personality. I received support from my partner Ana, and even went out on the town in Scheveningen, a Dutch seaside resort near The Hague famous for its nightlife.

Eventually, the Euros began and I was forced to watch from the sidelines. It was a difficult experience, but I learned a lot from it.

At the recommendation of the sports psychologist working with the team, I decided to attend one of the matches at the Euros. It was meant to be a way to get back into the mindset of the game, similar to getting behind the wheel of a car as soon as possible after an accident. I agreed with the suggestion and chose to go to the semi-final match against England.

However, it quickly became apparent that this was a grave mistake on my part. It was simply too early for me to be in the stands as a spectator. I should have been on the pitch, or at the very least on the sidelines as part of the coaching staff. My presence in the stands only served as a painful reminder that I should have been out there competing with my teammates.

My conversation with Merel had a lasting impact on me. It made me rethink how we announced the final team selection, as we needed to consider the feelings of both the chosen players and those who didn't make it. We wanted to ensure that those who didn't make the cut could leave straightaway and that we looked after their well-being. On the other hand, the players who made the team could celebrate their relief and savour the moment together. This conversation was far from easy for both of us. Thankfully, we were able to put it behind us at a later point and we continued working together for many years.

Merel van Dongen, Leeuwinnen defender

Playing football has always been a source of enjoyment for me. The period around Euro 2017 in the Netherlands taught me a lot. Once the tournament had ended, it was time for pre-season training at Ajax. Everyone was competing for a spot on the team, which created a lot of uncertainty and anxiety. However, it was during this time that something changed within me.

In the past few years I'd been playing for coaches, such as my coach Sarina, to prove that I was good enough to be on the team, but I finally decided to put an end to that. I wanted to play for the sheer enjoyment of it, to have as much fun as possible during each game.

This turning point would not have happened if I'd been selected to play in the Euros. Although I'd experienced great success before, this marked a pivotal moment in my career.

In September that year, Sarina gave me a call. Despite the emotional difficulties I'd gone through, she expressed interest in having me in the squad for the World Cup qualifiers. Although many coaches might not have reached out in that way, Sarina did. She asked me if I'd be available for selection, but said she understood if I needed more time to mentally and emotionally prepare.

Later, the three of us – Sarina, Arjan Veurink and myself – sat down together once again. Finally, I had the opportunity to express my frustrations to them, to share what it all meant to me and how much being dropped from the squad had hurt. They responded in a positive way, acknowledging and understanding my disappointment. The conversation itself was straightforward, just as you'd expect with Sarina. But the emotions were genuine, and we reached a deeper level of understanding.

During that same conversation, I also suggested that they should never handle the final squad selection in the same way again. I proposed that they ought to clearly communicate the inclusion of players in the squad at an earlier stage, no longer allowing non-selected players to attend the final meeting, and ensuring that all players return home well.

Together, we decided to put it all in the past and start afresh. And that's how it has remained. Embracing non-selection for any team is difficult and painful, but it can eventually lead to incredible moments.

2

THE LEEUWINNEN TAKE EUROPE BY STORM

Euro 2017 was set to begin, and our team had made impressive progress in a short span of time. Despite our accomplishments, however, I felt like something was missing. In order to compete at the highest level we needed to have complete trust in each other, particularly when facing the immense pressure that comes from being the home team. I therefore decided to speak with the coaching staff about what was bothering me. As I suspected, Arjan Veurink and Foppe de Haan told me that not everyone was sharing everything they needed to and that some players were holding back important information.

Vivianne Miedema was one of the most influential players in the squad for Euro 2017, possessing a unique ability to determine the outcome of matches by scoring goals when needed. I had the privilege of witnessing her journey to becoming a top striker up close. Another remarkable aspect of Vivianne was her openness and willingness to express her opinions. It was time to take action.

Vivianne Miedema, Leeuwinnen forward

Finding a balance between the players' input and the coaching staff was crucial. During our training camp we'd have group discussions, and these were structured differently each time. The staff organised these talks and sometimes grouped us based on positions like forwards, midfielders and defenders. Other times, they focused on specific areas like the central axis, the left flank and the right flank.

We were mindful to limit the frequency of these discussions. Having group talks every day wouldn't be very productive, and it was more efficient to have short meetings that addressed specific questions and topics. We realised that players would get tired of listening after an hour or so, so that was also considered in our approach.

Sarina worked closely with a select group of key players who were leaders in the team. Before she became coach, a group of experienced players had grown closer and formed a strong central axis on the pitch, giving us better control during games. In 2017 we had a powerful spine consisting of Sari van Veenendaal in goal, Stefanie van der Gragt and Anouk Dekker as central defenders, Sherida Spitse and Daniëlle van de Donk in midfield, and myself as striker. We also had supportive players around us who understood their roles and were eager to learn from games and tournaments.

Sarina was excellent at sensing when we weren't on the same page and she would quickly resolve any issues through discussions with the team. Sometimes we had to compromise and adopt her way of thinking, but at other times she and the staff had to adjust their approach to ours. Arjan Veurink played an important role in facilitating these discussions, always ensuring that they were open, honest and straightforward.

Being willing to humble ourselves and adapt was crucial in these discussions. That's what I believe made them successful. It was all about finding a balance between the wishes of the coaching staff and those of the players. We all had to be willing to give and take so that we could bring out the best in ourselves on the pitch, and, ultimately, achieve peak performance.

DELIBERATE FRUSTRATION

The team was preparing to take a significant leap forward, but how should the players react when faced with such pressure? How should the team as a whole respond?

With a great deal of enthusiasm and excitement we put together our own version of the Euro qualifiers, holding a mini-tournament both on and off the pitch before the actual tournament began. Following each game, Arjan would take a photo of the winning team. The player who appeared in the most photographs would be crowned the overall winner. Naturally, our players were eager to have their faces in those pictures because, like any player, they always strove to come out on top.

Foppe took on the role of the 'appeals committee', giving players an opportunity to voice their grievances if they disagreed with the decisions of the referees, who were selected from our coaching staff. It's common for players to argue with refereeing decisions, but this time we intentionally allowed the refereeing to be even more flawed than usual. The players' frustrations quickly became apparent, and Foppe had a lot of work to do with the appeals committee. Everything was unfolding exactly as we had planned. In fact, it worked so well that I couldn't help noticing that I was getting increasingly frustrated with all the criticism. I thought, 'Great, now we only need another.'

Finally, the moment we had been anticipating arrived. For the third time in a row I intentionally blew the whistle against the attacking side, but this time the players were so agitated and so preoccupied with a sense of injustice that they lost focus on their individual tasks. Their intense emotions had gotten the better of their judgement, and it was clear that they weren't yet ready to fully trust each other in such situations as they didn't know each other well enough to possess that level of trust. It was the last day of that phase of the training camp, and everyone would be going home for a few days. We hoped that the players would reflect on these events and contemplate their significance.

Being a coach is an incredible thing. It's not just about the actual moments of gameplay, but also how we respond to them as players, coaches and staff. We had deliberately planned these strategies in advance with the coaching team: we wanted to put the team under pressure through a mini-tournament. We also considered what we could do in the following days to make the impact of our strategies even stronger.

Instead of addressing the issues right then and there, during the training camp, we took a different approach. The players and coaching staff had the weekend off. It was the perfect opportunity for them, and for us, to think about their frustrations in the comfort of their own homes. It was important to acknowledge the moment, and we created space for emotions and reflection at home.

During that weekend I spoke on the phone individually with several players about our experiment. We wanted to know what had happened and how they felt about it. It quickly became apparent that the players had had a tough time emotionally over the weekend. It felt like failure. How good in fact were they as a team? And why had they come up short?

I emphasised that this was a fantastic opportunity to elevate the team to new heights. We knew that the key to success is being able to perform under intense pressure, even when emotions are running high. Trusting in your teammates and fulfilling your roles while maintaining constant communication is vital, especially when playing on home turf during the Euros. I asked the players if they were willing to play their part in taking the team to the next level. And, of course, they were.

After the weekend we gathered for a team talk. I was eager to see how the weekend and the phone calls had impacted on the players. This was a crucial moment for the team's growth. These are the moments when, as a coach, you can make great strides forward with your team.

I was fully focused and well prepared for the meeting. The most nerve-wracking part for me was when and how the players would share their thoughts with me. But I didn't have to wait long. Shortly after I started the team talk, without any prompting the players joined in the conversation. It was exactly what I was hoping for from the leaders in the squad, and it was both fulfilling and significant when one by one they shared their thoughts.

Sari van Veenendaal and Anouk Dekker opened up about their feelings and expressed their willingness to contribute to the group. Before long, the other players also joined in and shared their perspectives.

The players openly acknowledged that they could have done better in the mini-tournament, and because some of them were so honest and open about their experiences, something significant and meaningful was starting to emerge. We worked together to analyse the root causes of their frustrations, how their communication style had changed, and why they hadn't stayed focused on their roles within the team.

Over a period of just a week the players had learned that they could cope with the challenges of intense pressure. After all, we were playing the Euros on home turf, so it was a given that the team would be subject to immense expectations and that unforeseen things would occur.

It's only natural that as you progress further in a tournament, the pressure builds up. You expect to feel uncertain, unsettled and nervous at times – in fact, it would be quite strange if you didn't. However, you can still keep playing football by staying focused on the present moment, sticking to your tasks and following the game plan on the pitch. You can always give your best and put in everything you've got. That way, your teammates can rely on you. By embracing this mindset, communicating your uncertainties, finding solutions together and staying focused on the task at hand, a team can build a stronger level of trust and organisation.

At that moment, through this approach, I believe we managed to alleviate some of the pressure on the team. Of course, our ultimate dream was still to win the Euros. But what were our chances? History suggested that our chances were not great. But as long as there was a chance, we were ready to take it. We might succeed, we might fail, but if we gave it our all, we could be proud of what the team had achieved.

We couldn't control the quality of the opposition, but we could prepare as best as we could. We could only give our utmost effort as a team, both on and off the pitch. And that's exactly what we did.

Lieke Martens, Leeuwinnen forward

What struck me later about the Lionesses – I'm talking about the England women's national team here – was how familiar everything seemed from our time together with the Leeuwinnen. Sarina Wiegman, our coach at the time, had a set group of key players that she relied on. She had a clear idea of her starting line-up and rarely deviated from it. Even if I had an off day and didn't perform up to my usual standards, it didn't have immediate consequences. Sarina continued to recognise my abilities as a player and show confidence in me. I truly admired that about her.

Sarina knew how to emphasise the importance of the entire squad, not just the starting XI. She understood each player's role in the larger picture, especially during crucial matches. Her style of communication was always clear and open. Of course, she has grown and evolved in her role over the years, but her clarity fostered a deep respect among the players.

During Euro 2017 the dynamics within the team were excellent. Both the players and coaching staff were on the same page, we performed well and genuinely enjoyed each other's company. However, even in such a positive environment Sarina didn't shy away from making tough decisions. Sarina is a compassionate person who wants the best for everyone. But being the coach of the Leeuwinnen meant she had to make difficult choices, even regarding players she had worked with for a long time, like Merel and Mandy. These decisions weren't easy, but she made them because she knew it was in the best interests of the team.

We had an awesome group of women on our team, and the vibe was incredible. Being happy together was super-important, especially during a long tournament. We all felt comfortable being ourselves around each other. We played lots of games and joked around, which made everyone feel positive. Our success during matches felt effortless because we were all truly happy.

Since the Euros were being held in the Netherlands, we didn't have to travel much. We stayed in Zeist during the tournament's initial phase and moved to De Lutte for the semi-finals. Our mode of transport to each match was a bus. Our trusty bus driver, Mayke, had a go-to song she played every time we hit the road: 'Sunny Days' by Armin van Buuren. After the matches, we'd go back to our 'own' hotel beds. There was also time to spend with family. This was important for everyone, as having the support and love of your family can give you great peace of mind. Winning together and sharing victories with loved ones gave our team a massive boost, which made us even stronger. We didn't do this every day since we needed to focus on the games, but I tried to find a balance by linking family time to matches, and the players really appreciated it. Winning is important, but having the right attitude and support is just as crucial for success.

Lieke Martens, Leeuwinnen forward

The opening game of Euro 2017 against Norway was the first time we'd played in a big, packed stadium. We weren't used to having that many people watching us play, as women's football wasn't widely followed in the Netherlands at the time. When we found out that the fixture at the Galgenwaard stadium in Utrecht was sold out, it added to the excitement. Previously, the stands would mostly be filled with our families and friends, along with a small number of fans. But during the Euros everything changed. So many people were coming to support us at every game, which was an amazing feeling and created some unforgettable moments.

We were confident that we could beat the Norwegian team. They were good, but we'd already defeated them once before, which gave us confidence. We'd also lost against them, so we knew from the start that we needed to give it our all in the opening game. The goal I helped create was a special moment for me. I had the ball on the left side and saw Shanice van de Sanden making a run into the box, so I decided to cross the ball into her path. Normally, Shanice wouldn't head the ball that high off the ground, but this time she did. In games like this, spectacular things can happen. Some might call it luck, but we were also playing to win. By pushing ourselves and creating more chances, we were able to come out on top with a 1–0 victory against Norway. It was truly a dream start for us.

WE DO IT TOGETHER

It was an incredible feeling to win our first game, especially considering how challenging the first games can be. We were in a group with Denmark, Belgium and Norway, and while we believed we had the potential to defeat all three teams, it was important to prove it on the pitch. Now that we'd emerged triumphant in our first match, we began preparing for our next challenge against Denmark a few days later.

At the end of every team talk, I always emphasised our values, the values of the Leeuwinnen.

1. Stay in the present
2. Be united as one
3. Fight for it
4. Keep it simple = do your job = masterful performance

Our goal was to give our best possible performance. To stay true to these values, we frequently referred to them during discussions throughout the tournament and even backed them up with relevant videos. This required a huge amount of preparation time, but it was highly effective and so became a fixed routine in our talks.

GOOSEBUMPS DURING THE VICTORY PARADE THROUGH UTRECHT

A few weeks passed and we had some great wins against Denmark and Belgium. As group winners we faced Sweden in the quarter-finals and won 2–0 in Doetinchem. Next up was a semi-final against England, and we beat them 3–0, securing our spot in the final, in which we'd be taking on Denmark once again. It was exciting!

In the days leading up to the final we stayed at the Wilmersberg Hotel in De Lutte. We couldn't believe we'd made it this far. Before the tournament started we'd told the players that our chances of becoming European champions were slim, but we need to go for that slim chance. And now it was right in front of us. We were feeling confident and excited. Midfielder Anouk Dekker came up to me and said, 'Sarina, don't worry, we're definitely going to win tomorrow.' We knew it wasn't going to be easy, but her confidence gave us all a boost.

Denmark were familiar opponents to us, especially since we'd played against them in the group stage. They had a dangerous attacker in Pernille Harder, and midfielder Sanne Troelsgaard Nielsen was at the top of her game as well. One of the challenges was their deep-playing right-back. We wanted to avoid asking Lieke

Martens to handle her and end up playing as a makeshift left-back, which would be putting a lot of pressure on her. It was a difficult situation for the team.

Denmark scored early in the game when Harder passed to Nielsen on the right side and she was brought down in the penalty area. Less than six minutes had passed, and we were already one down following the successfully converted Danish penalty. All I could think was that it was early in the game and we still had plenty of time to make things right. Luckily, we managed to equalise quickly. Four minutes later, Vivianne converted a cross from Shanice van de Sanden, bringing us back on level terms.

Throughout the first half we were increasingly able to more attacking opportunities on our left side. Then in the 27th minute Lieke Martens received a central ball from the right several metres outside the Danish box, turned, took a few steps and curled a long-range shot into the bottom right-hand corner with her left foot, putting us into a 2–1 lead. However, Denmark quickly demonstrated their resilience once again, and Harder showcased her class by scoring a solo equaliser, making it 2–2 just four minutes after we'd gone ahead. It was all even at half-time, and the game could still go either way.

What stands out from the second half is how the game continued to ebb and flow. With chances for both

Denmark and us, the tension remained high for a long time. Shortly after the break, we took the lead again thanks to a free kick from Sherida Spitse. Denmark kept putting pressure on us and had several chances to equalise, but with two minutes of normal time remaining Vivianne received the ball on the left side of the pitch, cut inside, and with a powerful shot low into the near corner she sealed the game, making it 4–2.

Foppe de Haan came down from the stands to the dug-out excitedly proclaiming that we'd won the title. The only thing I could tell him at that moment was to sit down, because anything could still happen. That's how I always think when we're ahead just before the end of the match, but also when we're behind. It's not all over until the final whistle. Fortunately, that came quickly. The game was over, and we were European champions!

We successfully created a football spectacle with the Netherlands. The odds of becoming champions had seemed so slim, but our belief grew stronger with each game. This team possessed incredible strength, and our joyful energy resonated with the fans, leading to a remarkable connection. It was an experience that will never be forgotten. However, the most extraordinary moment was still awaiting us.

THE CANALS OF UTRECHT: A VICTORY PARADE TO REMEMBER

The most amazing moment of my year in 2017 was after the Leeuwinnen won and we had our victory parade in Utrecht. At that moment we finally realised that there was a lot more going on in the Netherlands outside of our football bubble. We felt an incredible sensation of freedom and excitement now that we could unwind and enjoy our victory to the full. One of the best parts of the parade was going through Utrecht's outer ring of canals on a barge to reach Park Lepelenburg.

Honestly, we had no idea what to expect that day, but we were mostly looking forward to it. We saw helicopters hovering above us, and we had drinks and music on board. The canals were packed with people standing three rows deep and some were even jumping into the water! Then we turned a corner and saw a sea of fans dressed in orange. It was such an incredible experience, one I'll never forget. I was filled with emotions that day because I realised what we'd achieved, what we'd unleashed in the Netherlands and what it meant to everyone in the country. It completely changed my life.

I suddenly had a flashback to the opening game, when we still had the entire tournament ahead of us. It felt like a whole movie played in my mind, from when I was a girl not allowed to play football to now becoming European champions. The whole of the Netherlands was on cloud nine. Many people were wearing the national team shirts with our players' names on them, and there was a lot of excitement, with everyone screaming and clapping. The players were being cheered on and hailed as heroes. Shanice van de Sanden, one of our forwards, had always said that we'd win the tournament – and that moment was now here. We'd achieved the impossible. Not many people believed we could become European champions, but we proved them wrong. The relief and the realisation that we had done it felt incredible. It was an amazing feeling for the fans, players, staff and myself. It couldn't have been any better.

I enjoyed watching the celebrations from a distance. It was fantastic to see how much the players were enjoying the moment, and the coaching staff were having a great time too. I was proud of everyone and showed it, although I made a deliberate decision to stay in the background that day and savour these precious moments from afar. I was there as the coach, and it wasn't my job to be a cheer-leader, although if I'd been a player I'd have certainly danced and sung along with everyone else. On the barge there was a magnum-sized bottle of champagne. As we rounded that final corner I told Niels de Vries, our exercise physiologist, that we should open the bottle and toast our victory. That was when I briefly danced and waved in the foreground, until I noticed the cameras starting to focus on me and I returned to be with my staff.

We had achieved our dream, and it was a moment worth celebrating. However, we couldn't bask in the glory for too long as the first qualifying match for the 2019 World Cup in France was coming up very soon.

Before we started to prepare for the World Cup, there were other matters I had to attend to before we could focus on the tournament in France. In the same way that I expect a lot from my players in terms of their professional growth, I hold myself to exactly the same standards. Euro 2017 taught me how much responsibility comes with being a national coach. It was a turning point that made me realise the need to develop professionally. However, after the tournament I found it challenging to say no. I also struggle when it comes to handling negotiations, and it was inevitable that discussions and negotiations would follow the Euros once again.

I first met Pauline Siemers when she was press spokesperson for the Leeuwinnen. We enjoyed an easy understanding requiring just a few words, and that was crucial for me as I prefer people to be on the same page as me. Back then, Pauline was setting up Sparkling Orange, a sports agency focused on managing communication. She was working with Lienke van Santvoort, and I immediately got along with Lienke as well. We decided to team up because I needed someone to manage a whole range of things for me as the coach.

Lienke van Santvoort, Sarina's management team

The relationship between Sarina, Pauline and myself is unique yet completely natural. In fact, the three of us are all pioneers in our respective roles. We prioritise emotions rather than relying solely on our experience in the football business. Over time, and built on a foundation of honesty, we've grown to know each other extremely well. Pauline and I may have different personalities, but that dynamic works in our favour when we support Sarina. We understand her wants and needs, and the areas in which she requires assistance. Financial negotiations and arrangements are tasks she happily delegates to us. Additionally, we handle various daily enquiries. Sometimes, Sarina reaches out to discuss more challenging issues or simply to vent her thoughts and frustrations.

Before I reached out to Pauline and Lienke for assistance, my sister Diana was the person who organised many things for me. Despite having a full-time job at

BMW, she gladly helped me handle all the enquiries coming my way. However, when things became overwhelming, I had a conversation with Diana about adopting a different approach. It turned out that she was completely onboard with the idea. Although she was deeply invested in my work and enjoyed contributing to it, we managed to find a balance. She had a busy schedule with both her work and her family but she still took care of certain tasks for me, while Pauline and Lienke handled the rest.

Pauline Siemers, Sarina's management team

We haven't improved Sarina's coaching skills because she's always been at the top of her game. However, we have helped her manage the business side of things. Being a national coach and 'celebrity' involves much more than people realise, but we try to make it all run smoothly for her. We explore opportunities and choices, including commercial contracts and ambassadorial roles with organisations like the Johan Cruyff Foundation and Plan International. Requests for Sarina to give presentations come in from all over the world, but due to her busy schedule, she can only do them a few times a year at most. As a result, we now have to attach a commercial price tag to these engagements.

I was learning to let go of certain things. Most importantly, Pauline and Lienke assisted me in establishing boundaries and understanding the pressures involved, often much faster than I could. As the approaching World Cup drew near, those pressures were building up.

3

THE WEIGHT OF EXPECTATIONS

UNDERSTANDING THE SIGNIFICANCE OF BEING THE FAVOURITE

In 2017 we came out of nowhere and won the Euros, but even though we still had to qualify for the 2019 World Cup in France, people were already predicting that we'd become the next world champions. They didn't have a clue.

There's a lot of comparing of men's football with the women's game. Thankfully, women's football is getting better, but we can't ignore the fact that it simply hasn't been around as long as men's football. It's also worth saying that just because Canada aren't that highly regarded in men's football, it doesn't mean the same applies to their women's side. Likewise, the United States have reached the semi-finals of the men's World Cup once (in 1930) and the quarter-finals once (in 2002), but the USWNT are always a strong favourite to win in the women's version.

During the six weeks of Euro 2017 a lot changed. The players suddenly became household names in the Netherlands. Now everyone had an opinion about the Leeuwinnen, the coaching staff and women's football in general. The media, who were usually focused on the men's game, started looking at women's football in the same way. They became more critical, and it took some getting used to.

We'd set a goal with the players to ensure we weren't just one-hit wonders, but we had to adjust to the fact that we were now in the sights of other top national teams, rather than doing the targeting ourselves. Suddenly the expectations were much higher. Some players handled it well, others struggled. They needed time to adapt to their newfound status.

Lieke Martens, Leeuwinnen forward

Because of our success at Euro 2017, everyone back home had high expectations for the World Cup in 2019. People in the Netherlands believed we would be crowned world champions in France. It's typical of the Dutch to think that way, to believe that after an unexpected success we would easily win an even tougher tournament. However, Europe is filled with strong national teams, and the World Cup brings together even stronger ones. Countries like the United States, Brazil and Canada all had a realistic shot at the title. And European teams knew that we were a tough team to beat, which presented them with an extra challenge.

A lot more changed as well. Suddenly, we'd become a team with many so-called head coaches. Everyone had an opinion about us, knew our strengths and weaknesses, both as individuals and as a team. The media and social media blew our performances out of proportion. The outside world decided who was good and who wasn't. It was the first time we'd experienced this level of attention. During the Euros, everything had been smooth sailing and fantastic, and as a player it had been great to read about it. But at the World Cup it was quite the opposite. We were not prepared for this, and it had an impact on the team and on individual players.

That year I made a decision to read less about what was being written about me in the media. I realised that it didn't help me stay focused on the tournament. By not reading the articles, I didn't have to spend time dealing with comments, whether positive or negative. In 2017 my friends and family had sent me lots of articles. To start with these were mainly about football, but after the Euros there was more and more stuff about my personal life. At that point I asked my friends and family to stop sending me media reports – I simply didn't want to see them anymore. That decision worked well for me.

Similar to our approach during the Euros, we made the decision to avoid placing too much emphasis on the final outcome in our external communications. Instead, we directed our attention towards defining our dream, acknowledging the challenges and outlining the steps to make that dream a reality. I've learned from experience that constantly fixating on the result can create a breeding ground for fear of failure. It fails to provide concrete guidance on what actions are necessary for success. By shifting our focus to taking action, we stay in the present moment and actively address the 'how'.

We began our journey to the World Cup by picking up where we left off during the Euros. Our team was in great form, creating a lot of chances and playing to packed, enthusiastic stadiums at home in the Netherlands. Our first opponent in the qualifiers was Norway, a challenging team who we'd beaten in the first match of Euro 2017. Although we couldn't put away any of the many chances we had in the 90 minutes, we were confident as we'd given few chances away, apart from a penalty that was stopped, thanks to the great work of Sari van Veenendaal. In the third minute of injury time our confidence paid off with a goal from Vivianne Miedema. The final score was 1–0, and it was a great way to kick off our route to the tournament.

NOT GOOD ENOUGH

We didn't always enjoy such good fortune, however. Our final game of 2017 was another crucial World Cup qualifier, this time against Ireland. It was important for us to end the year on a high, and we came into the match with good energy levels. Once again we had numerous chances to score, but we simply couldn't find the back of the net. We gave it our all, yet there was always something blocking our way – an arm, a leg or the crossbar. I wasn't too worried with a draw at full-time because we played a good game. However, the points we dropped against Ireland had a bigger impact on us than I initially realised.

Fast forward to 4 September 2018 and the final qualifying game for the World Cup against Norway, in Oslo. We knew that Norway were strong opponents. Although we'd already defeated them 1–0 in our opening home match in Groningen, they'd also been performing well in qualification. Because of our draw against Ireland, a draw was sufficient for us, while they had to win the match to secure a spot in the World Cup finals, something we were fully aware of. We needed to be completely focused from the very first minute of the game. However, during our training camp before the match I noticed that we weren't at our best, not giving it our full 100 per cent.

Everyone had the upcoming World Cup on their minds, including the marketing and communications department, who were busy preparing the campaign for the tournament. It felt as if the focus was too much on other things, and we still had to play the actual game to get us there. As team coach I tried my best to get a handle on things both inside and outside the team, and given the quality of our opponents we knew we needed to have complete focus.

Unfortunately, our performance in the match wasn't good enough and things went wrong from the very beginning. We were sloppy in one-on-one situations, we weren't working well together and within ten minutes were 2–0 down. We managed to find our rhythm towards the end of the first half, and Vivianne Miedema scored a goal to bring us back into contention. After the break we dominated the game in their half but failed to score. In the end we suffered a 2–1 defeat, meaning we didn't qualify directly for the World Cup. Now we'd have to play two rounds of play-off matches in our attempt to qualify and show that we were not simply a one-day wonder.

I'd already sensed at the training camp that the same level of focus, quality and connection that I was used to was missing. Something needed to be done. That's why I decided to travel around Europe to visit our players and speak with them individually. I went to England, France and Spain to discuss what had happened before and during the game against Norway. What did we need to do to ensure we didn't lose focus in the next game? What could the players do to help bring this about, and what did they need from us to achieve this?

During our next training camp, we started things off as usual with a full group meeting. As we began, several players immediately took responsibility for their short-comings. They identified what they felt was missing, and what they'd not been doing enough of. Some players mentioned a lack of interaction with others during a specific training session, while others admitted that they hadn't given it their all when needed. In some cases, play-ers realised that they'd failed to communicate with their teammates when things got tough, and this caused a rift between them.

These honest moments were accompanied by a strong belief in our mission. It was incredibly powerful to witness our players embracing vulnerability, taking responsibility for their own performances and committing to self-improvement for the sake of the team. This pivotal moment marked a significant turning point for the team and validated my investment in the trip around Europe to visit each player individually. In times of difficulty and potential conflicts, the players understood the importance of seeking each other out. By doing so, they fostered a deeper understanding among themselves, and in turn I better understood them.

We approached the playoffs with determination, aiming to secure a spot in the World Cup. Overcoming various challenges, we celebrated victories against Denmark and Switzerland. As we headed to France, our team had the confidence and belief that we were not mere flashes in the pan.

Lieke Martens, Leeuwinnen forward

When she was coach of the Leeuwinnen, Sarina had a strong character and wasn't easily influenced by other people's opinions. She stuck to her way of working after 2017, which helped protect the team from the intense and increasingly critical media attention. Within the team, there were players with good relationships who could support each other when needed. Additionally, there was always a sports psychologist available for consultation if necessary.

In 2017 Sarina had already proven herself as a prominent figure in women's football. Over the following two years her profile only grew stronger. This was especially evident during the 2019 World Cup, where she confidently and calmly explained her choices in response to questions from the media, helping to bring calm to the team.

Sarina, along with the press manager and coaching staff, effectively managed the media, and they also provided guidance on handling social media. Players and staff were free to decide how they wanted to interact with platforms like Facebook and Instagram. It was a personal choice, as some players enjoyed reading the reactions, using them to enhance their World Cup experience, while others preferred to avoid them and closed their social media accounts. It was important to establish ground rules and give everyone the freedom to approach it in their own way.

WILLPOWER AGAINST JAPAN

We started our 2019 World Cup campaign in France in a group with Canada, Cameroon and New Zealand. We won all three games, ending up as Group E winners with all nine points.

In the round of 16 we faced Japan in what turned out to be a game of two halves. Japan was feared as tough opponents after we struggled against them during the

2015 World Cup, but this time around we felt confident that we could take them on.

During the first half we played exactly as we wanted to as a team. We lined up in a 4–4–2 formation and focused on shutting down Japan's wingers to create a 3-against-2 situation. This enabled players like Jackie Groenen or Daniëlle van de Donk to support our attacks and outnumber Japan's defence. If the opponent tracked our player, we would have one player more in the axis and the line to the forward would be free. We worked together brilliantly and played them off the park.

After reviewing a lot of game footage, we found one attack that stood out. It had everything we wanted to see: players filling different areas of the pitch, moving in opposite directions to maximise efficiency and creating scoring opportunities. We were so impressed, we revisited it in subsequent sessions to inspire the team and focus on the positive aspects of our strategy.

The first half of the game was absolutely fantastic. We played some excellent football and should have scored more goals. However, things took a turn for the worse in the second half when Japan did something different. They decided to stay in their formation and keep their wing players in position.

This new strategy created a lot of uncertainty for us during our attacks, and we lost possession frequently and unnecessarily. Japan patiently waited for us to make a mistake and then swiftly counter-attacked. We were on the edge and living dangerously.

We needed a different approach at that time. It was crucial for one of our wing defenders to position themselves beyond Japan's outer midfielder. This strategic move would have created an advantage in our build-up and forced Japan to make decisions. Unfortunately, that scenario didn't unfold, which left us feeling uncertain. It wasn't because Japan were suddenly outperforming us, but primarily because they chose to take a defensive stance. We lacked a solution in that moment. As the coach I also struggled to provide the team with the guidance they needed. Communication with the players proved to be challenging.

So it truly was a game of two halves. In the first half we played brilliantly but missed out on converting more chances. In the second, Japan became more dangerous and had several good opportunities to win the game.

As the match drew to its conclusion it became all about belief and willpower. We truly believed that we were a tough team to beat and had confidence in our ability to prevent goals with our strategic positioning on the pitch. These foundations had carried us far in the tournament. Additionally, we were convinced that we could always score goals, thanks to our fast attackers and outstanding midfielders like Sherida Spitse and Jackie Groenen, both excellent distributors of the ball.

Our willpower was fuelled by the fact that we were still in the battle to make it to the next round, the quarter-finals. We also had a stroke of luck on our side when the Video Assistant Referee (VAR) intervened to confirm a handball committed by a Japanese player after the referee had given a penalty. The moment that followed will forever be etched in my memory. Lieke Martens stood on the spot, holding the ball, surrounded by four Japan players attempting to distract and unsettle her in the hope that she would miss. Lieke remained composed and determined, with a steadfast expression on her face. She knew deep down that she would score.

Lieke Martens, Leeuwinnen forward

In the round of 16 game against Japan, I scored my first goal of the tournament. It was an exciting moment for me, and it gave me a huge confidence boost for the rest of the game. Towards the end of the match, just before the final whistle, striker Vivianne Miedema took a shot that was blocked by the hand of one of the Japan players, resulting in a penalty being awarded to us.

When it came to penalty kicks, Sherida Spitse was always at the top of the list. However, in that moment I felt a strong conviction that I should be the one putting the ball on the spot. I approached Sherida and asked if I could take it, for no other reason than my own certainty that I'd score. I felt an intense urge to step up and take responsibility. Given how well I'd been playing in the game, I wanted to seize the opportunity.

But first there was a VAR check to confirm the decision. Those seconds felt like an eternity. I held the ball in my hands and my only focus was on retaining my concentration. I created my own little world, shutting out everything around me, even though it felt like I was being surrounded by ten Japan players.

My deep concentration paid off, and I stroked the ball in to the right of the keeper. The score was now 2–1 in our favour, and we secured a spot in the quarter-finals.

After the intensity of the Japan game, we continued our winning streak by beating Italy in the quarter-final with a stunning 2–0 victory. This not only secured our spot in the semi-final but also earned us qualification for the Olympic Games in Tokyo. Originally scheduled for 2020, the Games were postponed to 2021 due to the Covid-19 pandemic. The thought of competing in the Olympics gave our team an extra surge of motivation throughout the tournament. But before we could even think about that, we had to face the challenge of our semi-final against Sweden.

Our semi-final was against Sweden, with a crowd of 60,000 filling the stadium at Olympique Lyon. Half of the spectators proudly wore orange, and we discovered that the entire nation of the Netherlands was tuning in for our game during prime time. The level of anticipation was sky-high. At that moment our team was buzzing with excitement for the upcoming semi-final, although worries loomed over Lieke's injury.

Lieke Martens, Leeuwinnen forward

From a sporting point of view, the World Cup was quite a wild ride for me. I wasn't 100 per cent because of a toe injury. I'd been dealing with it since the beginning of the tournament, and with the number of games we played back-to-back it only got worse. After the group stage, the pain became even more intense. However, I was determined to push through and give it my all, with the adrenaline helping me play through the discomfort. I wanted to be able to look at myself in the mirror and know that I'd given everything I had at the tournament.

Before and after each game I'd a lot of contact with the medical staff and talked to Sarina. After the group stage game against Japan I could barely walk. In fact, I only played during the matches, not in training. I was given painkillers, but once their effects wore off after the game, walking became difficult again. The day after the game it improved a little, and I had two days before the next match. I spent a lot of time on the bike and in the fitness room, trying to recover. During that time I watched training sessions from the sidelines, sitting on a stool, hoping that I'd be able to play in the next match without holding anything back. Before each game I was given painkillers. Stepping onto the pitch for the warm-up always made me nervous because that's when I'd find out how much pain I'd feel.

Throughout the entire tournament I felt that Sarina had complete confidence in me. We spoke with each other frequently, and I was honest with her about what I could contribute in the upcoming game. However, for the semi-final against Sweden, things weren't going well. I told Sarina that I was in too much pain, and she asked me to give my all for 45 minutes – just the first half. The bond I'd formed with Sarina as my coach was so strong that I'd do anything for her, and I was willing to do whatever it took to win the World Cup. It was important for me to communicate with Sarina about my capabilities so that I wouldn't hold the team back in any way. She could then decide if it was enough, or if she needed to start with another player.

Together, we pushed me to my limits. Considering the severity of my injury, I couldn't do more than that. But I was able to finish the tournament knowing that I'd given it my all.

I'd announced the starting line-up for the semi-final, and ahead of the match we were feeling confident and purposeful. Although Sweden were tough opponents, we were familiar with their style of play and knew that we'd have opportunities to score. Before the game I watched our players in the hotel and noticed a combination of focus, composure and confidence among them. As the match approached, the tension grew, but being together as a team provided the necessary relaxation. Some tables were filled with louder laughter than others, but it was evident that the players were enjoying themselves.

I looked over to Merel van Dongen as it was a significant moment for her. She'd missed out on Euro 2017, but now had the opportunity to start in a World Cup semi-final.

Merel van Dongen, Leeuwinnen defender

During the World Cup there was a moment when I realised something important: the Leeuwinnen could win even with me on the team. This realisation only came after the semi-final, which left me feeling on edge and anxious while sitting in the hotel before the final game.

On the day of the semi-final, I was really nervous. I struggled to eat as I normally do. Despite having more experience since my first World Cup in 2015, I found it difficult to get food down knowing that I'd burn over a thousand calories during the game ahead.

Although being with my teammates was a helpful distraction, my mind was constantly on the upcoming contest, which was set for 9 pm. We were confident in our ability to stop Sweden from scoring, and we knew what we had to do. As a defender, being part of a team that possessed such flow was an incredible feeling.

When the referee blew the whistle for the game to start we had 30,000 fans behind us, a truly exhilarating moment. In the first 15 minutes every pass I made seemed to end up with the opposing team, but suddenly I found my rhythm. It felt like someone had given me an extra boost of energy, as if I had an oxygen tank on my back. It was an incredible game to be a part of. Even towards the end of extra-time I didn't feel any exhaustion. I felt as if I could play another game if needed. What an amazing feeling.

When Jackie Groenen scored the decisive goal in the 99th minute I'd a strong belief that we were going to win the game. It was a defining moment that signalled our journey to the final was under way.

A SURPRISING GAME PLAN IN THE FINAL AGAINST THE UNITED STATES

After defeating Sweden in the semi-final, our focus immediately shifted to the United States. They were the reigning world champions and incredibly strong opponents, with a powerful attack. We had already extensively analysed their strengths and weaknesses, which highlighted players like Megan Rapinoe and Alex Morgan as key threats. Consequently, we decided to start with our strongest defenders, meaning that Merel van Dongen had to sit on the bench despite having started against Sweden.

In an interesting coincidence, my colleagues Arjan Veurink, assistant trainer Michel Kreek and I all independently came up with the same strategy to exploit the weaknesses of the American team. We anticipated being forced back deep into our own half, so we planned to take advantage of the moments of transition. Throughout the World Cup we'd regularly used a triangle formation up front, with Vivianne Miedema, Daniëlle van de Donk and Lineth Beerensteyn. However, our plan was to surprise the United States by positioning this triangle differently and starting Vivianne in midfield. This adjustment would allow us to quickly transition, use Vivianne as the first target player and play into the space behind their defence with Lineth's speed. We believed this approach could effectively disrupt their defensive midfielder and central defenders.

In the final our plan worked surprisingly well. Although the United States team were indeed formidable, we'd given them too much respect. Despite this we had a number of chances early in the game, but then a penalty was awarded. That was unfortunate but our fatigue played a part too. It had only been three days since our intense semi-final match, which had gone into extra-time. Meanwhile, the United States had an extra day of rest, adding to their already strong performance.

Megan Rapinoe successfully scored the penalty, putting them 1–0 up. We could sense that it would be incredibly difficult to turn the game around. The fatigue weighed heavily on the team, and unfortunately, substitutions couldn't change the pattern of the game. Although we had come closer to beating the US than ever before, it ultimately wasn't close enough, with Rose Lavelle scoring another for the Americans in the 69th minute. We had to settle for second place as the runners-up.

4

BOTH SIDES OF THE COIN

As we prepared for the 2020 Olympic Games in Tokyo, our goal was to continue developing our team. As the coach, I wanted our playing style to constantly improve. After the 2019 World Cup in France, we focused on strengthening the squad during training camps and matches. We had a strong foundation, and once that foundation was solid enough we tried a new approach, progressing through a series of developmental steps: from unconsciously incompetent, to consciously incompetent, to consciously competent, to finally becoming unconsciously competent. As the team internalised these concepts, so our thinking went, we'd be able to take our performance to the next level.

CONFINED IN TOKYO

At the very height of the Covid-19 pandemic, the Olympic Games were postponed for a year and rescheduled for 2021, when they'd take place under strict safety protocols. This unexpected delay gave us an unprecedented opportunity to continue making significant strides in our development and progress towards excellence.

During training the first step in our new approach went well. The players became aware of their shortcomings in executing the team's build-up play, just as we'd asked them to. However, we didn't have the opportunity to take the subsequent important steps. We'd made our players so conscious of their need to improve the basics that they became uncertain and struggled. Training became challenging, and I even reached a point where I had to accept that the perfect developmental strategy might not work in the run-up to the Olympics. The discomfort that we experienced impacted on our matches.

Anja van Ginhoven, former Leeuwinnen press officer

We were incredibly excited about the Olympic Games in Tokyo. Being part of the Dutch team added a whole new level of significance. The Leeuwinnen would be part of the grandest sporting event on the planet, and if we won in Japan it would be yet another milestone for women's football in the Netherlands. But then out of the blue, Covid-19 changed everything.

The tournament was a surreal experience for us. I'll never forget the feeling of being locked up in our hotel in Tokyo, restricted to a dedicated section of the building and isolated from the public areas. Our only entrance was through the rear door, which was heavily guarded by at least six security personnel. They made sure we went straight to our rooms, so it felt like we were in prison. We couldn't go outside, and our movement within the hotel was heavily controlled. We were essentially prisoners at the Olympic Games.

Unbeknownst to us, our confinement turned out to be a valuable exercise in team development. It was crucial for the team to find some kind of release valve for our frustrations. Sarina set the tone when she addressed the issue of athletes needing more freedom with the IOC during a press conference following our win against Zambia. Unfortunately, her concerns fell on deaf ears.

Back in the hotel, we decided to push the boundaries and find some humour in our situation. During meals, there were glass screens separating us at the dining table. It wasn't long before I was one of the first to remove the screen dividing us. The team understood that we were doing everything we could to maximise our performance in the face of challenging circumstances. But despite being at the Olympic Games, it just didn't feel like we'd all imagined it would be.

Our second game in the group stage was against Brazil, a team I always look forward to meeting as they have a highly explosive forward line and a dynamic set of players. At the 2019 World Cup we rarely conceded goals, but the same couldn't be said for the Olympics. There were moments when our defence was vulnerable, and this became all too evident in our second group match against Brazil. While we scored easily, we also conceded too many goals. The final score was 3–3, a result that presented us with the next challenge to solve.

RHYTHM AND ROUTINE

In our last group game we played China, beaten at a canter 5–0 by Brazil in their first match. We were level on points with Brazil and they played Zambia in their final game, whom we'd convincingly beaten 10–3. It was fairly obvious that both Brazil and us would make it to the quarter-finals, the only question being who would finish in first place and be more likely to play against the United States – who finished second in their group – in the quarter-finals. We knew the United States well from the 2019 World Cup final.

Sometimes coaches face difficult choices in football tournaments. What should you do when you've already made it through to the knockout round with a game to spare, or what if you can avoid a strong opponent in the next round by playing a certain way – and trying to lose – in your final group game? Coaches have tried different things in the past few decades, like resting their best players or slowing down the game to get a better result.

I've never believed in that kind of thinking. Football is about winning games, not doing maths. You can never predict what will happen in the future, and that's precisely what makes sports so exciting. While it's nice to plan ahead, it's all about winning today.

As a coach, I like to keep things consistent. If a team goes too long without playing together they can lose their rhythm. That's why I always try to field pretty much the same team in the final group game, unless someone is injured or gets a yellow card. Sometimes I'll give a player who's close to being a regular starter a chance to play. But I don't want to make too many changes and I want to keep the rhythm.

We were now convinced that we could beat the United States. Moreover, our other opponent in our side of the draw was most probably going to be Canada; they were also very good, as shown when they ultimately won the Olympic title. At the time I thought Canada had made a better start to the tournament than the United States, so it was certainly not a given that we'd easily beat Canada.

Imagine if we'd let China win our final group game, and we'd then lost to Canada. We'd worked together for seven years to achieve something great, so we weren't about to let ourselves be knocked out like that. Giving it our all against China was also about who we were and what we wanted to represent. A month later we were invited to have lunch with King Willem-Alexander, and he brought the subject up. He joked that we should have just lost to China after all. Of course, I simply couldn't agree with him.

We eventually came out 8–2 winners against China. Brazil only won 1–0 against Zambia, so as the top team in our group we had to face the United States, who'd finished second behind Canada in theirs. We were looking forward to it – the only dark cloud on our horizon at the time was that our hotel accommodation resembled a prison!

Lieke Martens, Leeuwinnen forward

We'd heard from many who had been to the Olympics before us that it was a unique and special experience, but unfortunately it was not as positive for us as we'd hoped and I don't think many of our players will look back on it with fond memories. The staff did their best within the limitations they faced, but it felt like we were trapped in our hotel, and there were so many restrictions due to Covid-19. We tried to push the boundaries by going outside, but the heat was unbearable. We even put up a dartboard, but it was taken down without our knowing. Things weren't made easy for us.

The players and staff tried to make the best of our situation, but it was just so difficult. We couldn't open the windows in our hotel rooms, and there was no way for us to contact our families while in Japan because of restrictions on communication. Even having video calls was a challenge on account of the significant time difference between Japan and the Netherlands. If we had a game in the evening, it meant we were stuck indoors for the whole day. Normally I don't care for pre-game rituals, but in Japan I really missed going out for a coffee with the rest of the team on game day.

OUR CHANCE TO BEAT THE UNITED STATES

Playing top-quality football during tournaments is an incredible feeling and it quickly became our way of escaping the feeling of being confined. This time, when facing the United States, we approached the match with a different mindset. We were confident in our ability to win this quarter-final and go all the way in the tournament, drawing on our experiences in the World Cup final and the friendly match we played against them in November 2020. We truly believed that this was the moment when we'd finally come out victorious.

Vivianne Miedema, Leeuwinnen forward

After our disappointing loss to the United States in the 2019 World Cup final, we were determined to find a way to defeat them in the future. We knew we had the potential to beat them, and the coaching duo of Sarina and Arjan came up with an idea: pushing our defenders further up the pitch. It was a brilliant strategy, especially considering the strength of our offensive players, but it did mean that there were times when we'd have only three players defending instead of the usual four.

We decided to test out this new strategy in several games leading up to the Olympic Games in 2021. It quickly became evident, however, that pushing our defenders forward didn't allow them to showcase their strengths. This approach introduced greater risks in defence. After the games, we had discussions with both players and staff. We collectively felt that we were not comfortable adapting to this style of play and that it was not bringing out the best in us.

To address this issue, Sarina and Arjan worked with us to adopt a different strategy for our matches at the Olympics. That's how we started our matches at the Olympic Games.

We knew the United States would come at us hard from the beginning of the game, and they did just that for the first 20 minutes. Vivianne Miedema, who'd been scoring effortlessly throughout the tournament, gave us an early 1–0 lead. With Arjan there alongside me, I couldn't help but notice how flawless our build-up play was in this game, even under immense pressure. Suddenly, the players were no longer afraid to play with conviction when bringing the ball up from the back and developing play.

Because they were trailing, the United States continued to attack relentlessly, scoring twice in just three minutes to take the lead at 2–1, but we kept our composure and grew stronger as the game went on. In the second half, Vivianne struck again to bring the score level at 2–2. With over half an hour to go, we knew we had a chance to score another and win the game.

In the 80th minute we were awarded a penalty, and Lieke Martens stepped up to take it. We'd practised penalties beforehand and had agreed on our strategy. I had complete faith in Lieke to make it count, as she had a history of scoring crucial penalties in the past. But unfortunately, it wasn't meant to be, and we headed into extra-time with the score still at two apiece. The tension in the air was palpable.

Lieke Martens, Leeuwinnen forward

We knew that the United States would come at us hard in the first 20 minutes of the quarter-final of the women's tournament in the 2020 Olympics. Our game plan was designed to handle that. In the first half we took a more cautious approach than usual, to break down their play. So it wasn't a coincidence that we took a 1–0 lead at the end of the first 20 minutes with a fantastic shot by Vivianne Miedema. However, we ended up trailing

2–1 at half-time, conceding two goals in just three minutes.

In the second half I felt that we were much the better team than the United States. We played with less caution and created a lot of scoring opportunities. When Vivianne scored a second goal, we believed that we had more goals in us. We truly were the stronger team, and after Sarina substituted Lineth Beerensteyn for Shanice van de Sanden, one of her first moves led to a penalty for us. This was the crucial moment, the chance to decide the game in the 80th minute. As in the 2019 World Cup game against Japan there was a VAR check. I chose the same corner I had in that match, but unfortunately I missed, and the score remained 2–2. The game went into extra-time and then penalties to determine who would advance to the semi-finals.

This game was different from the World Cup final between the same two teams two years earlier. The United States were the reigning world champions and the team to beat. At the time, we were proud of how far we'd come. Some tournaments require you to grow, to get closer to being the best team. For that reason, we approached the Olympics with a different mindset. We believed that the United States could be beaten this time, but it didn't turn out that way. We lost on penalties, and suddenly it was all over. It was a real missed opportunity; we could have been Olympic champions, but too many of our players weren't in top form. When that happens in elite sport, you get sent packing.

It was a tumultuous end to the game. In extra-time three times we believed we'd scored the winning goal but the VAR disallowed every one of them. Eventually it all came down to penalties. Unfortunately, luck was not on our side and we ended up losing the shoot-out.

The pain this time was almost unbearable. We believed, no, we knew we had what it took to win. We'd wanted to play two more games and finish our journey with a gold medal. And then the realisation slowly began sinking in. We'd been eliminated, and this was my last game with the Leeuwinnen. It was time to pack up and go home. Saying goodbye to the Leeuwinnen was incredibly difficult, and I had little time to process it all. The Lionesses were waiting for me.

5

FROM LEEUWINNEN TO LIONESSES

In August 2020 the English and Dutch football associations issued a joint statement announcing my appointment as the head coach of the Lionesses, effective after the Olympic Games in Japan, which had been postponed until 2021. While I was excited about this opportunity, I couldn't ignore the fact that I still had a significant year ahead of me with the Leeuwinnen, and I was looking forward to the Olympic Games immensely. In the football world it's quite unusual to announce a transfer of this magnitude so far in advance.

However, the chance to become the head coach of the Lionesses was too good to pass up. The Football Association had made a significant investment in the women's game, and with the impending Euros in 2022, and England as the host nation, it was an opportunity I couldn't resist. The Lionesses had access to the same FA facilities as the England men's team, the Three Lions. While the FA had already put many organisational pieces in place, they gave me the freedom to put everything in place that was necessary for success at the Euros. For me, this has always been an important precondition for starting anything.

I just knew it was the perfect time to become the coach of the Lionesses. The team had a lot of talent and potential, and they were hungry for success, but they hadn't won any major championships yet. The Lionesses had made it to the semi-finals in the last three major tournaments, but had always fallen short. It was a source of collective disappointment for football fans in England, who had not witnessed a major championship victory by any of their national teams since 1966.

But things were looking up. I had great memories of playing in front of my home crowd during the Leeuwinnen's successful run in the Netherlands in 2017, and it was both thrilling and challenging to be offered the opportunity to make a difference with the Lionesses on their own turf in 2022.

But as the Olympic Games drew near, I, of course, had my loyalty to the Leeuwinnen: the team, the staff and the football association. Together we'd embarked on an incredible journey over the past few years, one that had been intense and unforgettable. After our triumphant performance at the Euros and our great run at the World Cup, we were eagerly anticipating the Games. For me, my mission with the Leeuwinnen would not be complete without the Olympics. It felt like we were approaching the finishing line together, not just for me, but for the players and staff as well.

However, I knew that news of my upcoming departure would have a significant impact and garner widespread media attention. With the Olympics just around the corner, we couldn't afford any distractions. So, we decided to make a media announcement at an even earlier stage to minimise any disruptions in the lead-up to the Games.

The FA faced an additional challenge, with Phil Neville, the previous head coach of the Lionesses, having already announced his departure. During my talks with the FA I raised this topic with Sue Campbell, the director of women's football. She had a clear vision for how to navigate this issue.

Baroness Sue Campbell DBE, FA director of women's football

Leading the team had been a challenging experience for me, especially given Phil's decision to join David Beckham at Inter Miami in the American MLS, and Sarina's commitment to the Leeuwinnen for the Olympics. As a result, I'd no choice but to appoint an interim manager for six months, although I knew that two managerial transitions in quick succession would disrupt the players and hinder their progress. I had to weigh the potential disruption against the added value of Sarina's arrival. Ultimately, I concluded that the benefits of having Sarina as our new coach outweighed the potential disruption caused by the managerial transition.

We'd already engaged in multiple discussions with Sarina, alongside another candidate who was also well suited to the job of coaching the Lionesses, albeit for different reasons. One of the factors that set Sarina apart was her emphasis on a 'team-first' mentality as a crucial part of her vision. Having known our players for a long time, and having watched many of them develop from youth players to professionals, I believed that they deserved a coach who could take them to the next level of success. This was not a revolutionary change, but rather an evolution towards greater achievements. Sarina was the perfect match for this role, as she clearly communicated what she thought was necessary to make this next step.

During our conversation, I looked at Sarina intently and praised her for her player-centred approach and vision for team development. However, I also probed further and asked her a crucial question: 'How important is winning to you?'

There was a twinkle in her eyes that went beyond anything that she could say with words. I shall always remember that twinkle. There was also an energy that I could feel and see, and it left a lasting impression on me. Since that moment, I've been fortunate enough to witness that same sparkle on several occasions. Sarina possesses a unique combination of a winner's mentality and a deep desire to succeed, while also understanding that it takes team effort to achieve success. Like me, she takes great pleasure in bringing out the best in her players. Sarina isn't someone who craves the spotlight; she derives great joy from the growth and development of others. I knew that we had made the right choice.

ADAPTING TO BRITISH CULTURE

I knew that moving from the Leeuwinnen to the Lionesses would also mean I'd be immersing myself in a new culture. That was one aspect of this new job that really excited me. Years earlier I'd had the opportunity of playing football – soccer – in the United States, which was a valuable experience for me that enabled me to explore a different sporting culture. And likewise with the Lionesses, I was curious to see what my experience would be like.

Early on, it was made clear in the Netherlands that I'd be leaving for England after the Olympic Games in Tokyo.

This gave me more time to prepare for my new work environment, and I could openly discuss these preparations since everyone already knew about the job. However, in reality, I'd a limited amount of time in which to do so as I was completely focused on the Leeuwinnen at the Olympics.

I decided against taking a crash course at the Language Institute Regina Coeli, known as 'the nuns of Vught', due to time constraints. Instead I opted for private lessons with an English tutor who specialised in football. My English was already decent, partly thanks to my time in the States, but I specifically wanted to brush up on football-related terminology. In the end I had 12 one-hour lessons, but it was challenging to fit them in to my busy schedule. Nonetheless, my constantly improving English proved to be extremely beneficial during my initial interaction with the England players, including Jill Scott.

As I got to know Jill, I discovered her to be a dedicated and determined player who always gave her all for the team. She would go on to play a crucial role in making our dream with the Lionesses come true at Euro 2022.

Jill Scott, Lionesses midfielder

Normally, I'm someone who easily connects with people I haven't met before, but when I first met Sarina it was different. Despite not being being the tallest person in the room, she had a captivating presence. Of course, I was aware of her impressive success with the Leeuwinnen, and if I'm being honest I was a little apprehensive. This had to do with her straightforward way of communicating.

In England we're more accustomed to trying to make people feel comfortable by cracking jokes and having a laugh. But from the very beginning, Sarina was extremely direct and made it clear what she expected from us as a team. For me it took a while longer to get over that and introduce myself.

What happened next was also remarkable. When we first met it felt like Sarina had been a part of our team for years. Normally, there's some tension in the air when you stand in front of a group for the first time. But there was none of that. She'd done her research and had a good understanding of each of us. She'd already outlined her plan for the upcoming months and had complete confidence in it. The choice was to go along with her plan. However, her plan was so well thought out and appealing that there was actually no choice to be made. Sarina knew that and radiated that belief. In this way she set the standard for all the meetings, training sessions and matches that followed.

To get a better idea about English football I had many conversations with people who closely followed the English game, Dutch people who had worked in England and English people I knew personally. One aspect of British culture that I wanted to learn more about was forms of politeness and etiquette, which were considerably different than those in the Netherlands.

In order to communicate effectively, I wanted to get to know British culture as quickly as possible. I needed to be on the same page as the staff and the players, and I knew this would require some adjustments, not just on my part but on theirs as well. First, I focused on my own cultural acclimatisation. I read several books that mentioned how specific expressions in the Netherlands had a quite different meaning in Britain. For example, the phrase 'okay' in Dutch is quite positive, but in Britain it can sometimes carry the connotation of reluctance. In English the phrase 'that's interesting' can be used to suggest that you don't care in the slightest for something, while in Dutch it expresses curiosity. To avoid misunderstandings, I tried to learn as many of these differences as possible before my official start with the FA.

Later on I'd learn other expressions. For example, I attended a match with Anja van Ginhoven, general manager of the Lionesses, shortly after we started. After the game we spoke to a number of people, including Sue

Campbell. At the end of our chat she asked if we'd like a meal at her place. This presented a dilemma to us. We wondered whether she was asking out of British politeness or if she really wanted a meal with us to continue the conversation. We pondered this for a while but ended up declining the invitation. A week later we enquired about it, and it turned out that we'd have been welcomed with open arms. It's a funny example, but it made me realise how delicate and sensitive language can be.

Another significant cultural difference I encountered was the sensitivity of the players and staff towards hierarchy. In the Netherlands it was common for staff members to express their opinions openly and directly during meetings. However, the context was different there because when I started as head coach I'd already been working with everyone for some time; it wasn't like starting afresh as a new coach. But in England things were different. I was introduced as a top coach who had reached finals and won an international trophy. This meant that during the first staff meetings, people would listen to me as the head coach and anything I said was immediately taken as being the solution.

At this particular moment I deemed it important to listen carefully to different players. Lucy Bronze was one of these. She is a highly experienced player who'd already acquired a considerable array of medals and awards, including the 2020 FIFA Player of the Year Award. When I started my job in England, Lucy was injured and she only joined us later. Our initial meeting was a bit awkward and we needed more time to get to know each other and build up a bond of trust. Since then things have gone swimmingly.

Lucy Bronze, Lionesses defender

Sarina is not a wizard like Harry Potter and she doesn't have a magic wand with which to perform miracles. When she became the coach of the Lionesses there was already a strong foundation. We had a talented squad capable of winning tournaments, and we always had a positive mindset, winning games and playing great football. Sarina had seen this from the very beginning.

In the past we had coaching staff who provided clarity in their goals but couldn't create an environment that brought out the best in us. On the other hand, we also had staff who we could challenge, but they lacked the clarity we needed to collectively achieve our objectives. Sarina was able to find the perfect balance and achieve success. The major difference was that now we had an environment where we felt comfortable challenging each other, and it was clear to everyone what Sarina expected of us.

But because I believed it was important to consider everyone's points of view before coming to a decision, I needed to change my approach somewhat. Instead of immediately sharing my own opinions, I started asking the staff a series of open-ended questions. These questions didn't lead them towards my own opinion but encouraged them to support their own opinions with reasoning. That way we could have collective discussions and make more informed decisions. It took some time for both the staff and myself to adjust, but the quality of our solutions significantly improved.

Because I was outside of my comfort zone at the KNVB, in England it was one of my personal goals to establish connections with people and make the best use of their qualities. I wanted to adapt and adjust to a different culture in order to develop a shared understanding and reach the highest level together. By doing so, we would maximise the chances of reaching our dream.

I can't help but chuckle a bit when people put me on a pedestal because I'm not one to boast about myself. It's said that you shouldn't believe too much in your own abilities, but luckily that wasn't a problem for me. It was exciting to join the Lionesses, especially with the finals of the tournament taking place on home turf. However, after that, it was all about rolling up our sleeves and putting in the hard work to perform at our best as a team. All I could do was give it my all, pedestal or not, together with the staff.

Geraint Twose, Lionesses assistant coach

I learned a great deal from Sarina, and working with her helped me grow as an assistant coach. I could sense her confidence when I was preparing training sessions. Before each session I'd present my plan and receive feedback from her, then we'd go out on the pitch and start the session. Sometimes we had to make adjustments along the way, but because we were so well prepared we could do these quickly and effectively.

Our interaction during training sessions had a positive impact on me. I always felt comfortable and instructed, which enabled me to develop as a coach. This was mainly because of the professional relationship we had, focused on bringing out the best in our players and staff.

Sarina's clarity regarding our playing style helps my organisation as I can plan the session with the detail that develops both our style and individual players. This planning is important as it maximises our work with the players. Sarina often jokes about how early I go to the pitch to set up the session, but when the players walk onto it you want it to be the best experience for them every single time.

I'm now much more conscious of how vital it is to get important tasks done in a timely manner, such as planning training sessions or preparing video clips. I've structured my planning around this, and I've found myself making fewer last-minute changes.

As a coach, the beginning of your tenure with a new team is the perfect opportunity to shape the set-up to your liking. When I finally joined the Lionesses after the Olympics, I took my time and carefully observed how the organisation operated. While I'd formed a mental image of it based on the discussions I'd already had, those first few weeks were crucial in refining my assessment of the organisation through my own observations. I engaged in numerous conversations, making sure that I struck a balance between approaching the fresh faces and the experienced members like Geraint Twose, who'd been a part of the FA for a considerable time.

Geraint Twose, Lionesses assistant coach

Sarina and I were supposed to meet for the first time before our first training session. That meeting was just like how our partnership developed over time. I got to know her as a passionate and competitive coach who holds herself, her staff and her team to a very high standard. She sets us challenges and supports us in achieving them, and she's interested in the people she works with.

For me, Sarina is the type of leader you want to follow because she's inspiring, not only with regards to football but also in how she works with people. During our first meeting I felt appreciated, and what pleased me most was the balance between challenge and support to bring out the best in me. Our short introductory meeting turned into an in-depth conversation that lasted for 90 minutes, and we ended up walking onto the training pitch still talking with great animation.

By and large, the FA had already established a competent and professional structure. Football occupies a special place in England, being the cradle of the sport, and this is reflected in the investments made in the women's game in recent years. However, I wasn't entirely satisfied with the working methods and effectiveness of the coaching staff. I attempted to gain a comprehensive understanding of the organisational structure, workflow and consultation processes, but I still had unanswered questions.

Using my observations and overview, I created a rough outline of how I envisioned things working. Success could only be achieved if everyone, both on and off the pitch, performed to the highest standards and had a clear understanding of their roles and responsibilities. I shared my rough outline with Arjan Veurink, who would come with me to the Lionesses, and discussed the content with him. Like no other he is able to create a clear framework of responsibilities, roles and consultation structures. Prior to our first training camp, I presented this plan to the FA, who gave it their full support, even if it meant facing resistance from some staff members who were resistant to change.

At our first meeting, we explained our proposals to the staff, which brought much-needed clarity to our operations moving forward. The majority of them were pleased with the changes, as there had been a high turnover rate in personnel and this new structure restored a sense of stability. However, as time passed, it became apparent that not everyone was able or willing to adapt to our new way of working. We eventually had to reassign some of these individuals to new positions, but with the remaining staff we were able to achieve the level of excellence that was necessary. It was proof, however, of how Arjan and I complemented each other.

Arjan Veurink, Lionesses assistant coach

After spending four and a half years with the Leeuwinnen I felt it was time to move on to the next chapter of my career. I had a strong desire to work in a different culture, surrounded by different people and customs. It seemed like a valuable experience to broaden my horizons. Joining the English FA was an appealing opportunity for me for multiple reasons. Not only would it mean that I'd be joining a more professional organisation than the KNVB, but it also excited me to have the chance to improve my English-language skills. The future is unpredictable in the world of football, but I was confident that working at the FA would open doors for me and boost my career prospects. My ultimate dream has always been to become a national team coach, and being part of the FA would undoubtedly bring me closer to that goal.

After Sarina began her discussions with the FA, she asked me to come along too. We still had a great working relationship, but we both knew that this move would bring a new dynamic to our partnership. This meant that I'd take on further responsibilities within the team, while Sarina's status would rise to being head coach with overall responsibility for the entire team.

As we started our journey together, one of our first tasks was to improve how the team worked together. Sarina shared what she believed was important, and based on that I created a clear and straightforward structure and workflow for the team. This way, everyone knew exactly what they needed to do, and what their roles and responsibilities were. We divided team management into two parts. On one side general manager, who would oversee business support, marketing and commerce. Later Anja van Ginhoven would be appointed to manage this side of things. On the other side I focused on the technical aspects of football. Sarina led the entire team, taking overall responsibility, and she also managed the medical team.

What caught my attention in those first few months was the squad's transformation on the training pitch. The players trained with a very high intensity right from the off at our first camp, and they rarely complained or made excuses. This genuinely surprised me, and at first I thought it might simply have been an act to make a good impression on the new coaching staff. But as time went on it became clear that this was their new normal, and it worked exceptionally well. As a result, we were able to push the team further and get even more out of them during our training camps.

In the Netherlands it's quite straightforward to gauge what's happening within the squad. The players freely express their thoughts and are not afraid to be critical. The advantage of this is that previously unspoken processes quickly come to light, although it sometimes takes time. In England, however, it's a whole different ball game, and I find it fascinating. I'm interested in why is it so different here, and how we can open up more easily about the things that matter in England.

TEAM UNDER HIGH PRESSURE

As the first training camp with the Lionesses drew near, Arjan and I were eager to meet the team so that we could begin forming our initial impressions and assessments. We were determined from the outset to put football and the team centre stage. We had discussions with all the players, and we wasted no time in implementing our football vision during training sessions. One player who truly appreciated this approach was Ellen White. We could use her energy and positivity on the pitch.

Ellen White, Lionesses forward

Sarina was the coach the Lionesses had long been waiting for. She was unquestionably a top coach with a proven track record of winning major trophies in women's football, and I was deeply impressed by her achievements with the Leeuwinnen.

When she began with the Lionesses, it was evident to both the players and the staff that she was a competent and confident leader. Her exceptional skills and excellent communication approach were unparalleled in our prior experiences. From the moment we met her, it was clear that she had a burning desire to elevate our game to the next level. She took a keen interest in each and every one of us, both as athletes and as individuals, and this personal touch made a huge difference.

In one-on-one conversations with Sarina and Arjan, we had the opportunity to share our personal stories and backgrounds, and what drove us to succeed. This level of engagement and attention to detail was exactly what we needed to thrive as a team, and it paid off.

Sarina's background as a PE teacher proved invaluable when she shared her football vision with us. Whether in individual meetings or team talks, she was always crystal clear about the kind of football she wanted us to play. Her vision was tantalising, and we were eager to put it into action both as a team and as individual players.

Another key advantage of having Sarina as our coach was her extensive experience in women's football. While football is football, there are subtle differences between the men's and the women's game that require a coach with specific expertise. Sarina's wealth of experience in this respect was evident in her engaging coaching style, and it helped us immensely as we worked to achieve our goals.

Working with Sarina as a striker was a breath of fresh air. Her footballing vision was clear and structured, with a distinct plan for when we had possession of the ball. She drew a distinction between defenders and defensive midfielders on one hand, and attacking midfielders and forwards on the other. This allowed for more freedom and creativity for the forwards and creative players, which was a welcome change for me.

When the opposition had possession, we knew exactly what we had to do. We played a high line and pressed aggressively as a team, often regaining possession in the process. If that didn't work, we'd revert to our original shape. In each game we could fall back on known patterns of play and situations we had practised in training. This was all down to Sarina – no two ways about it.

During our first training camp we held individual sessions with each player to discuss their thoughts on what had made the Lionesses successful in reaching the semi-finals in three tournaments and what was necessary for the team to take the next step. These were open discussions that provided us with valuable insights that helped us immediately begin our work.

The first few weeks with the Lionesses went by in a flash as I quickly adapted to the customs, traditions, work schedule, team selection and staff. It was a demanding period, so I made a conscious effort to regularly visit my family in the Netherlands. Not only did this give me a chance to see them, but it also provided an opportunity to reflect on my work style. One of the things that stood out for me just after I became involved with the England set-up was my first casual conversation with goalkeeper Mary Earps.

Mary Earps, Lionesses goalkeeper

When I first had a conversation with Sarina I had serious doubts about whether I wanted to continue playing football. I felt like my glory days were in the past, and I'd lost my ambition. But talking to Sarina brought about a shift in perspective. She expressed her confidence in me by referencing specific situations in matches I'd played the previous year. It was clear that she had done her homework and knew what she was talking about. She mentioned moments that I struggled to remember myself. She saw a potential in me that I couldn't see in myself at that time.

What struck me the most was Sarina's honesty and direct way of communicating. It was like a wake-up call for me. I realised that there was still more to achieve and that I had the capability to reach new heights. Sarina's belief in me ignited a spark of determination that had been fading. Her words gave me the motivation to continue pursuing my football career with renewed vigour.

The conversation I had with Sarina and the goalkeeping coach was emotional. In the past I'd found it hard to trust people due to a lack of honesty in communication, and this made me consider quitting football altogether. However, when I met Sarina at the first training camp, everything changed. She was very clear about her goalkeeping selections and the order in which they would play. With several goalkeepers being unavailable due to injury, she mentioned that I was one of her first choices to start in the next match. I was shocked and emotional. It felt like I'd suddenly been promoted from being a goalkeeper who never played to being in the starting line-up.

Sarina was also honest about the future. She couldn't guarantee that I'd always be selected for future games, but she reassured me that she'd always tell me where I stood. Other goalkeepers were returning from injury, but I'd been given a chance to prove myself – and she was willing to give me that opportunity.

I didn't have any expectations. All I could do was show up, give it my all and work hard. Sarina's message to me was simple: 'You're Mary Earps. Just be yourself. That's more than enough. I've seen what you can do.'

No matter what happens in the future, I will always be full of respect for how Sarina helped me with my career. Sarina gave me the chance to fulfil my wildest dreams.

We won the Euros and I was honoured as the best goalkeeper in the world. I've won more trophies and awards than I ever imagined possible, and I hope this success continues for a long time to come.

The most important takeaway was that while the Lionesses had the talent to win, they had not been functioning as a cohesive team when under pressure. Players tended to focus on their individual games, and some even admitted that they hadn't always been supportive of one another.

To address this, I arranged for Dr Kate Hays, a highly respected sports psychologist, to join our staff, as I believe that working on psychological factors is crucial for teams playing at the highest level. Ahead of our first meeting with Kate I'd prepared a presentation outlining my vision for the role. To my surprise she'd also independently prepared a similar presentation. As we spoke, it quickly became evident that we shared the same perspective.

Kate Hays, head of women's performance psychology

Kay Cossington, the technical director of women's football at the FA, contacted me to talk about sports psychology for women's teams. As I spoke more with Kay, and we discussed what psychology could look like, I became more excited about the role and the possibilities for the future. She mentioned that Sarina, the coach for the women's team, wanted to interview me. However, when we met, it felt more like we were interviewing each other.

From that very first meeting, Sarina and I hit it off. We shared similar ideas about high-performance sport, and I could tell that Sarina had a strong football philosophy. She was determined to achieve success with her team, and I appreciated her single-mindedness. Despite her strong focus, Sarina had a warm and charismatic personality, which made it easy for her to connect with others.

Over my 20-year career, I've had the opportunity to work with some of the best coaches in the world. From my experience, I've learned that great coaches are also excellent psychologists. In time, my role has evolved from directly working with athletes to helping coaching staff enhance their approach from a psychology-based perspective. When I met Sarina, I was curious to see how far she was on this development path as a coach. It quickly became clear that Sarina was one of the most developed coaches I have worked with when it cames to sports psychology.

This was crucial because we had limited time to prepare before the 2022 European Championship began.

For us to perform at our best, everything needed to align within my team. When it came to Kate, it all fell into place in terms of expertise and rapport. From the moment we met, I had complete trust in her. She consistently delivered high-quality work, shared my vision and provided valuable feedback, even when it challenged my point of view. These were crucial factors that enabled us to work together and let go when needed.

Together with Kate, we focused on team development leading up to and including Euro 2022. Our goal was to foster stronger bonds among the players, encouraging them to be open and honest with each other and to trust each other under intense pressure. We were all in this together, working towards a common goal in an elite sporting environment with the best facilities, and our first training camp provided valuable insights into what was important to our players and how they performed at their best. Kate was able to make an important contribution to this.

Kate Hays, head of women's performance psychology

The framework we used to guide the team had four main themes. The first was focused on why we were there, creating a shared purpose for everyone on the team.

The second was about who we were as individuals – players and staff alike. We aimed to understand each other at a deeper level, so we knew our values, our strengths and any areas for growth. This enabled us to build a strong connection and open up communication among the team.

The third was 'How do we play?' With the expertise and experience of Sarina and the staff, a strong vision was developed regarding the football we wanted to play with the Lionesses.

The fourth theme was 'How do we win?' I believe strongly in realising a collective dream. Our dream was to be champions at Euro 2022, and we focused on playing at our best under the most extreme pressure. We didn't want to focus only on winning but also on how we wanted to win. To achieve this, we made sure that the team had a psychologically safe environment to work in. Players were able to make mistakes and learn from them, thereby becoming better as individuals and as a team.

The 'How do we win?' framework was something I'd been developing over the last 20 years of my career. From the very moment that I presented it to Sarina and Kay, together we brought the framework to life. I'd never experienced that so strongly before.

What made our approach stand out was that it applied to the entire staff. We had a diverse group of coaches, some with years of experience at the FA, others who were new colleagues from different backgrounds and cultures. From the beginning it felt like a cohesive team, and that was because Sarina gave us clear goals, sharing with us how to create a high-performance environment and what personal values were important to her when working together.

Sarina believed in inclusivity for the staff, regardless of rank or role. There were over 30 of us in all, and Sarina made sure that everyone had an equal say in team meetings. There was no hierarchy among the different staff members, and we encouraged a whole range of perspectives so we could make informed decisions. To ensure a shared experience across the entire set-up we mirrored team-development sessions for the players, following the same programme and identifying our staff profiles, communication styles and more.

It was remarkable how clearly everyone understood their roles right from the beginning. Sarina's teams were highly organised, so any distractions were eliminated and we all had a common purpose.

While talking to striker Beth Mead, it became evident that football was her utmost priority. She expressed her enthusiasm for our training camp, because above all we were playing football. She thought that too much emphasis in recent times had been placed on players' fitness levels, with one particular training camp dedicated above all to fitness tests, which took up a significant amount of her time. That wasn't the case now – football was centre stage, and the physical data could be obtained from the training sessions and the matches rather than being tested for separately.

Beth Mead, Lionesses forward

The Lionesses were known for their impressive fitness levels. We dedicated a lot of time to sprinting up and down the pitch, but at times we neglected the football itself. Sarina, our coach, recognised this and introduced simple training exercises to improve our skills. One such exercise involved keeping possession of the ball within a square. Initially, we ran around the square with no structure or pattern, eager to impress our coach. However, we soon realised that our footballing skills were lacking. To address this, Sarina placed a cone in the centre of an imaginary grid and divided it into four smaller quadrants, with two players assigned to each quadrant. This provided us with a clear structure to work within and prevented us from simply running around aimlessly at full speed.

The choice of training camp in Southampton was well thought out. We stayed at a lovely hotel with a golf course attached to it. Sometimes these camps can feel restrictive, but Sarina gave us the freedom to enjoy ourselves within the limits of our responsibilities. On our afternoon off, with the sun shining, she told us we could do whatever we wanted, as long as we returned in a reasonable state and on time. This was a refreshing way of working, and we all returned promptly and in good shape. We even discovered that some of us were quite good at golf!

It was like a honeymoon period with our new coach. We had face-to-face meetings where she got to know us and we got to know her. We also played a couple of great games in front of enthusiastic crowds. It was an exciting new beginning for us.

'I DON'T GIVE A SHIT IF YOU MAKE MISTAKES!'

During our first training camp I made it clear that I'd do my best to immerse myself in British culture, but I wouldn't compromise on giving direct feedback. However, I also emphasised that this did not mean we had a strict regime that discouraged making mistakes. In fact, making mistakes is a crucial part of the learning process and essential for progress.

Shortly before the Euros we played a friendly match against the Leeuwinnen. It was an exciting game and a chance for me to reconnect with my former team and coaching staff. The day before the match, we trained in the stadium and the Leeuwinnen had their training session right after us. We had an impromptu reunion, as we knew the players quite well. There were lots of hugs and catching up with each other, which made for a heart-warming experience.

Despite the high spirits, the game against the Leeuwinnen was a charged match. They were the reigning European champions and a formidable opponent for England. We had analysed their structures, game plan, strengths and weaknesses, and identified the key players. Our own game plan was based on this analysis, giving us our strategy with which to beat them.

Unfortunately, we had a poor start in the first half – there's no other way to describe it. We fell behind to a goal by Lieke Martens, who headed the ball in from a corner taken by Sherida Spitse. It was an extraordinary moment, since Sherida was playing her 200th international match, but I wasn't too pleased at the time. Lucy Bronze managed to score an equaliser on the half-hour mark from a lucky cross that looped into the net. Despite this, there was a cloud hanging over the team.

When the referee blew the whistle for half-time I walked across the pitch to the dressing room, feeling that something needed to change. 'Girls!' I exclaimed. 'I'm not sure what weight is on your shoulders, but please shake it off. Go out there and take action. Take the initiative and don't be afraid to make mistakes.' I paused for a moment, wondering whether to use the word 'shit'. I decided to go for it. 'Actually, I don't give a shit if you make mistakes! Right now, we're playing not to lose. Let's play some football and go for the win!' We succeeded in this; in the second half we played freely. We had made a break-through.

Millie Bright, Lionesses defender (captain)

What I appreciated most about Sarina as our coach was her willingness to let us make mistakes. Right from the start she emphasised that we could only learn if we took risks and didn't have to worry about being punished for making errors. As players we always gave our best effort, but we were free to make our own decisions on the pitch. Whatever decision that was, she was always in control.

I realised there was a difference in how I played for my club compared to when I represented the Lionesses. When I played for my club, I had a lot of confidence and didn't stress about making mistakes. I wanted to bring that same mentality to the national team. Sarina allowed us to make mistakes and pushed us to play with a more expressive style. This not only improved my performance, but also lifted the whole team. We played without fear and genuinely loved our time on the pitch.

We dedicated a lot of time leading up to Euro 2022 preparing for the pressures of playing in a tournament hosted at home, and I was able to share my own experiences from working with the Leeuwinnen in 2017. Since we were performing well, we were able to recognise when the pressure was building during the tournament. Being aware of this enabled us to handle it better.

Players have told me that it helps that I stay calm myself. In turn, my calmness helps them to stay calm. Even in the dressing room before the final against Germany, I maintained my composure, which helped the players approach the game as just another match. It was no more than that. Every game was characterised by the same routine. Even when I was absent due to my Covid-19 infection, everything followed the usual pattern and the team followed their regular routine. The players were always prepared and never let anything catch them off guard. The team simply executed their strategies until they were told to switch to a new plan.

At that point, during the half-time interval against the Netherlands, there wasn't much point talking about tactics. More often than not, games are decided through sheer grit, determination and taking the initiative, even against the reigning European champions. I took Chloe Kelly off and brought on Beth Mead, telling her to up the ante and play without fear. In this game she had to use all her attacking skills, even if they came to nothing.

Beth Mead, Lionesses forward

As a player, Sarina's arrival was like a breath of fresh air. At the time I also had a new manager at Arsenal, so having two new managers meant starting with a clean slate. This can sometimes be effective because you're judged on what they see, without any preconceptions. Until that point I wasn't a first-string player for the Lionesses. From day one, Sarina was a blessing for me, not because she always picked me, but because she was clear about what she expected from me.

The first time I met Sarina was during the 2019 World Cup in France, with my former partner Daniëlle van de Donk. I was aware that she had won the Euros in 2017 with the Leeuwinnen, partly at England's expense, so it felt a little strange. Even back then she had the aura of a success-ful coach about her, and I was slightly nervous, although completely unaware that she'd be my coach a few years later. To me, she was a breath of fresh air because she was open about how the tournament was going for her.

To be honest, my first impression was that she always looked serious. Nowadays, I can joke about it with her and ask if she's angry or just looks angry. She always replies that she's not certainly not angry, it's just her 'focus face'. Now that I know her better, I'm aware that she's not angry when she looks like that. She's a fantastic woman who cares about her players and has a sense of humour. As a coach, she knows the right balance between focus, expectations, concentration and fun. For me, having a laugh and making jokes are important.

I noticed that my approach was refreshing for the England players. As I've mentioned before, I'm straightforward about my expectations and what I want. The Lionesses truly believed in my footballing philosophy. Right from the first training camp we established a shared philosophy. Together with the staff and players, we devised a plan to bring it to life. It took some time, but gradually it became our collective philosophy, embraced and supported by everyone. This brought us a sense of calm and confidence, something we desperately needed. There was more creativity to their game.

Beth Mead, Lionesses forward

Naturally, I can't reveal all of our footballing secrets, as we still have several tournaments ahead of us under Sarina's leadership. She is crystal clear about how she wants us to play, the team's shape and how to achieve our footballing objectives at the highest level. This means that we always have specific patterns of play to fall back on. Sarina always demands 100 per cent from her players, as well as from herself and her staff.

As a full-blooded winger and creative player, I felt liberated when Sarina told me that I was free to express my creativity on the pitch. This was possible because I'd internalised my role, the way we played and the defensive expectations she had of me.

Without a doubt, she brings out the best in me.

What I appreciate most is the way Sarina communicates. She is clear, consistent, and tells me exactly where I stand in the squad at any given moment and what I need to do to make the starting line-up.

As we prepared for Euro 2022 we had a friendly match against the Leeuwinnen. This game held special significance for Sarina, but in the first half we had a hard time. I was slated to come in as a substitute in the second half. During the break, Sarina gave us clear instructions about what she expected from us as a team, and from me specifically. Her lucid instructions and ability to alleviate the pressure from the team were incredibly inspiring at that moment. I felt no pressure and was able to execute our plan on the pitch exactly as we had discussed.

The second half against the Netherlands began on a better note, but sometimes a team needs a game-changing moment. That moment arrived in the 52nd minute when the Leeuwinnen were awarded a penalty, and Dutch midfielder Sherida Spitse had the perfect opportunity to give them a 2–1 lead. However, she hit the outside of the post and missed. Immediately after that, we launched a brilliant attack down the right flank, and Beth Mead steered one in from a Lauren Hemp cross to put us ahead 2–1. In just one minute, we went from nearly being 2–1 down to going 2–1 up!

The team experienced a renewed sense of energy, shedding the weight of the first half. The home crowd in the stands sensed this and cheered us on even more fanatically. The Leeuwinnen were unable to match our pace and had to make substitutions out of sheer necessity. Suddenly, nothing could stop us and the goals kept going in. In the end we won 5–1.

It wasn't just the goals but the difference between the first and second halves that we carried with us to the Euros. The team had experienced a win against strong opposition by taking risks and accepting that mistakes were part of the process. We, the coaching staff, had encouraged this mindset, both in the dressing room at half-time and through our efforts on the touchline. Moreover, this game took place on our home turf, with 30,000 excited fans in attendance.

The team's belief in our own ability only intensified, bringing us closer to our dream of winning. As coaches we could tell them how strong we were, but the team had to feel it out there on the pitch. And that's precisely what happened.

6

BRING FOOTBALL HOME

As of December 2018, it was clear that the UEFA Women's Euro 2022 would take place in England. The tournament was about to begin. All those months of preparation had to come together now, with the goal of receiving the coveted trophy at London's Wembley Stadium.

But that was still a long way off. Since England was hosting the competition, automatic qualification was secured. We were in a group with Austria, Norway and Northern Ireland in the tournament's initial phase. Our first game against Austria began auspiciously as we scored an early goal – the only one of the game – courtesy of Beth Mead in the 16th minute.

Next up were Norway, whom I'd faced several times before with the Leeuwinnen. They proved to be a tough adversary, but we managed to find the back of the net time and time again, clinching a resounding 8–0 victory against them. We then moved on to face Northern Ireland, who also couldn't break through our defence, leading to a 5–0 victory.

We'd won all three games, accumulating a total of nine points and scored 14 goals with none against – an impressive feat. As a result, we advanced to the quarter-finals as group winners, which bolstered the team's mood and confidence. We were determined to go for our ultimate dream.

Beth Mead, Lionesses forward

I can't single out one specific moment. The entire tournament was incredibly intense for me, filled with numerous significant moments. The first major highlight was during the opening game against Austria, which had special meaning to me because we played at Old Trafford, the ground of the club I supported as a child. It was truly a dream come true to step onto that pitch.

Opening games are often quickly forgotten, and this one was no exception. However, we did emerge victorious. In the 16th minute, Fran Kirkby played a through ball to me. I managed to put enough onto my shot to lift it past the keeper and across the line, making it 1–0. It wasn't our best performance, and the tension was palpable as we played in front of our home crowd. Being selected in the starting line-up by Sarina gave me a boost of confidence, which was crucial for me to score.

After we won the first game, some of the tension was lifted from the team. Our next match in the group stage was against a highly respected opponent: Norway. We knew it was going to be a tough one – they were strong physically, scored freely and rarely made mistakes. But surprisingly, it turned out to be the easiest game for us.

During half-time, Sarina came into the dressing room and admitted that she hadn't been expecting this situation. She simply told us to keep pushing forward and not let up. By then the score was already 6–0 in our favour. It was as if everything we touched turned to gold. In the end we scored a remarkable eight goals in that match, and I managed to put away a hat-trick. The atmosphere in the stadium was something truly special, and every piece of the puzzle fell perfectly into place. It's not often as a player that you get to experience such games in your career.

SPECTACULAR QUARTER-FINAL AGAINST SPAIN

In the quarter-final against Spain everything clicked for me, and the game was undoubtedly the most thrilling match of my coaching career thus far.

Before the game many people believed that we'd had an easy draw for Euro 2022, with Austria, Norway and Northern Ireland as our opponents in the group stage. However, that wasn't the case at all. In my opinion the draw was actually quite challenging because if we made it out of our group we'd have to face either Spain or Germany – two of the top teams in the world – in the first of the knockout games.

Earlier that year we'd played against Germany in the final match of the Arnold Clark Cup. Germany have always been a formidable opponent for the England national side and we needed to secure three points against them to win the tournament. During my team talk before the game I asked the players if they were willing to go all out for the win, even if the score were level. The team responded with absolute determination – 'We want to win the game!'

It was a crucial moment for the team, the perfect opportunity to execute our back-up plan in a big game. We made a strong start against Germany, taking a 1–0 lead with a goal from Ella Toone. However, the Germans struck back before half-time with a well-executed free kick from Lina Magull to level the score. The second half played out much the same.

With 15 minutes left on the clock it was time to put our Plan B into action. Millie Bright would move up the pitch, then we'd press forward aggressively and use both wings to create scoring opportunities.

Personally, I was fully focused during matches like this, but I also recognised the deeper significance of the moment. Going up against our arch-rivals, we were applying immense pressure with players who were prepared to take risks and seize the initiative. Our strategy had already proven successful, and now it was time to see the rewards materialise on the pitch. And it didn't take long. Millie Bright scored six minutes before the end of normal time, putting us 2–1 up, and as soon as we went ahead we reverted back to our original formation. In injury time Fran Kirby even secured another goal, making it 3–1. The elation among the players was overwhelming when the final whistle blew. I realised that the way we'd won the game meant more to everyone than had it been a bigger margin but an easier win. It had been meticulously planned, with input from the staff, rehearsal with a number of players and extensive discussion among the team. The outcome was a terrifically accomplished performance on the pitch. Football truly is fantastic, isn't it?

Jill Scott, Lionesses midfielder

Sarina always said how lucky she was to have inherited such a great team. Even though she was usually the focus of attention because of all the games we won, she always switched the focus to the team. She refused to take all the credit for herself and always said it was because of the team. When she was voted FIFA Coach of the Year in 2022, she told everyone she was so happy to work with such an amazing team. I noticed that she became more relaxed in the months we worked together.

Another thing that surprised me was her emphasis on building a relationship with the fans. I'd been playing for England for over 16 years and always thought that you had to win something before you could win the fans over. But Sarina saw it differently.

The fans were coming to the games to see us, so we had to thank them before the game. That meant clapping for the fans when we warmed up. It felt strange at first, but I could feel the reaction from the crowd. They appreciated the gesture, and it created a connection between the fans and us, the players. This resulted in more intense support from the fans, especially during difficult moments in Euro 2022. The fans' support helped us get through the tough times, and we couldn't have done it without them.

You can't talk about the Euros in England, our home nation, without mentioning the fans. The noise they made was unbelievable. The interaction reached new levels every game. I still get goosebumps today when I think about it.

After this great victory over a powerful opponent in the Arnold Clark Cup, we now had to repeat the same strategy when it truly mattered – at the Euros. The opportunity presented itself on 20 July in the quarter-final against Spain in Brighton.

The game could have gone either way since both teams were evenly matched. There were periods when Spain had the upper hand, but there were also times when we were in control. Before the game we discussed with the players the importance of sticking to our own style of play. Spain had been dominant against all their opponents, keeping possession of the ball with a nonchalant confidence even against strong teams. We knew that even if we tried to adapt our style they'd still have the lion's share of the ball, so we focused on playing our own game, applying a high press and holding on to possession when we could. The post-match statistics showed that we had a 48 to 52 per cent share of the ball, a triumph in itself as it reduced Spain's dominance.

In the 54th minute Spain scored, taking a 1–0 lead. In the 82nd minute Arjan signalled for us to implement Plan

B. Millie Bright moved higher up the pitch, and two minutes later Ella Toone scored a crucial goal. This boosted our confidence, and Spain began to falter. The game went into extra-time, and it was Georgia Stanway's decisive shot that sealed the victory with a score of 2–1. The feeling of joy was indescribable.

Millie Bright, Lionesses defender (captain)

As a player you can feel when a crucial moment is coming during a match. You can also sense when you're going to win the game. During the Euro 2022 quarter-final against Spain, even though we were losing 1–0, I believed we'd make a comeback. We'd practised this in the Arnold Clark Cup in 2022, so I pushed forward to try and create an opportunity. Maybe I'd end up in a scoring position, or perhaps one of my teammates would. We trusted in our game plan and knew that we'd get a chance to equalise.

One of Sarina's strengths is that our team knows what our Plan B is, along with what each player needs to do in that situation. In this game Plan B was all about getting a goal, still with structure, but ultimately we needed a goal. Sarina also knew exactly when to implement this plan. For me, it was the perfect moment to push up front. But I was also aware that, once we scored, I'd need to drop back into position to continue with our original game plan.

In that moment after the game I remembered the process with my team, from the very beginning: the effort we'd put in, all the time and energy invested in both the staff and each individual player in order to achieve the best possible performance. All the individual conversations and team-building sessions – as well as our participation in the Arnold Clark Cup – had come together and been worth it.

As I now cast my mind back to the Euros, our victory over Spain was pivotal with the self-belief that was sparked in the latter part of the second half, the determination that we were not going to lose and the sense that we were part of something exceptional. Everything we did was focused on achieving our ultimate goal.

David Gerty, head of women's football communications

Sarina's preparation both on and off the pitch is remarkable and consistent. How she prepares on the pitch is mirrored by her level of preparation off it. During Euro 2022 we always had different plans ready for various scenarios. For instance, during the quarter-final game against Spain Sarina quickly put her Plan B into action. We also had a communication strategy in place whether we won or lost. With the Lionesses behind by one goal the communications team were discussing a 'worst-case' scenario strategy until the 84th minute, at which point Ella Toone scored, and we were soon able to switch to our victory-scenario plan.

What makes Sarina such a great leader is that she grants professional freedom to those she trusts. She keeps a close eye on the key aspects, but she places trust in the expertise of her support team and rarely questions why something is necessary

But we weren't there yet, as in the semi-final we were up against Sweden at Bramall Lane in Sheffield. The excitement after the Spain game quickly shifted to the focus on preparing for the next match against Sweden. We were confident that we could win. Months of intense work together had led us to this moment, and we were determined to reach new heights. We were ready for it, even though Covid-19 was still a factor.

HOW FAR WILL YOU GO TO REACH YOUR DREAMS?

As the number of infections increased, I gathered together a group of key players. It was an unusual setting because that evening I asked everyone to meet outside and maintain social distancing. I explained my concerns to the group and asked for their opinions. It was now just before the semi-final, and family gatherings had been planned. I wanted to address the matter because it posed an increased risk of infection.

It was a real dilemma. Connecting with family was important, especially at this stage, and it had been a while since the players had last seen their loved ones. Some players who hadn't yet played or had played fewer games than expected emphasised that it was important for them to have contact with their families, but they also understood that they were ten days away from the moment that could change their lives. Ten days before they could stand on the pitch at Wembley and write history with the Lionesses. Together we wanted to eliminate the risk of losing players to infection. It was a difficult decision, and many of the players would later say that this was the toughest moment of the tournament.

But it was also a precious moment. The leadership group had shown their commitment. We made a joint decision to cancel any contact with their families. It was tough. For the team, it meant they had to find other ways to have fun, rest and relax. The decisive moment was when they truly realised how close we were to our goal, and it was this that led to a shift in their mindset. They'd given everything they had to get to this point, and despite it being tough they were willing to cancel their trips home to improve our chances. Our group meeting concluded in the gloom on a grassy field. We gathered the whole team together there and then and informed them of our decision to stay in our own sealed-off bubble

There had been other occasions when I supported the advice of the key players. In April 2023 we played the first-ever Finalissima against Brazil. Just before the final whistle Brazil scored an equaliser, which meant there would be a penalty shoot-out. Before the match the coaching staff had prepared a list of penalty takers in a specific order, but out there on the pitch the players felt that this order needed to be changed. I listened to them and decided to go with what they suggested, having full confidence in this change. Luckily, it had a positive impact on the penalty shoot-out, and we won the game and the trophy.

Geraint Twose, Lionesses assistant coach

With Sarina as our coach, we always knew her game plan. She set the bar high, and it showed in our quarter-final against Spain in Euro 2022. We scored an equaliser by implementing a different tactical scenario with Millie Bright. Once the scores were level, we knew we had a great chance of winning the match.

During our post-match briefing, after eventually going through to the semi-final with a 2–1 victory, Sarina asked why we hadn't pressured Spain in the three minutes after the goal. It was a real eye-opener for me. Regardless of what happened on the pitch, we were supposed to stick to the plan. We were so ecstatic about equalising that we forgot to follow through with what we'd agreed upon before the match. One lesson we learned for the semi-final was for both the staff and players to stay focused.

We'd experienced the same situation in the final game of 2022, a friendly against Norway. The media had hyped up the match because if we won, we'd remain undefeated for the entire year. We went ahead and scored, but with ten minutes left Norway equalised. At that moment Sarina could have settled for a draw to preserve our unbeaten status, but that was never her plan. She wanted to use the game to make some changes to our formation and stuck to her guns, even after the equaliser. We continued to put effort into attacking and trying to win the game, despite the risk of conceding a goal and losing our undefeated record. Luckily, the match ended 1–1.

On 26 July we faced Sweden in the semi-final. The winner of this match would go on to play in the final against either Germany or France, whose match was taking place the following evening. Sweden had secured their spot in the semi-finals by defeating Switzerland and Portugal and drawing against the Netherlands in the group stage, then beating Belgium in the quarter-final.

The atmosphere at Bramall Lane was electric, with nearly 30,000 spectators filling the stadium. The crowd's energy when the England players stepped out onto the pitch was simply incredible and we hoped that it would help contribute to a convincing victory.

As the game progressed, the excitement began to build. In the 34th minute Beth Mead finally scored the opening goal. Fourteen minutes later, Lucy Bronze made it 2–0 in our favour. After half-time, Alessia Russo got her chance to score with an amazing backheel through the Swedish keeper's legs, and a few minutes after that, Fran Kirby added another goal to our tally. We'd beaten Sweden convincingly with a 4–0 scoreline and now Wembley awaited us.

THE ENERGY OF A SOLD-OUT WEMBLEY STADIUM

The next day, Germany emerged victorious over France, setting them up as our opponents in the final. I'd been the national coach of the Lionesses for less than a year and this was the moment we'd all been waiting for. It was time for the England team to claim their first major prize.

Beth Mead, Lionesses forward

There are some coaches who communicate their message consistently for only a brief period, but Sarina possesses that rare quality of constantly communicating with her players. She'll check on you regularly, even when you're sidelined with an injury, enquiring about your well-being both on and off the pitch. This is a constant in her approach, whether you're playing or not. One of her greatest talents lies in her ability to keep her players calm, focused and primed for performance during the most challenging moments.

During the build-up to the Euro final we were all packed into the dressing room. As footballers, we're quite adept at making the game feel convoluted and complicated. Sarina, however, does the exact opposite. She simplifies and distils everything down to its essence. It was just another football game, and if we each carried out our individual tasks on the pitch there was a good chance we'd come away with the victory. It was such a straightforward approach, yet incredibly hard to execute in such high-pressure settings. But her words had a profound impact on us, instilling us with a newfound sense of confidence as we took to the pitch.

Of course, I felt the pressure. We were up against Germany, and we'd all watched their semi-final against France together. We were really impressed by them. I thought they were the toughest opponent we'd faced in the tournament, and they deserved to be in the final of the Euros.

What made this match even more significant was its historical context. The England–Germany rivalry had been iconic since the 1966 men's World Cup final. England won that match 4–2 in extra-time, including a legendary and controversial goal from Geoff Hurst that struck the crossbar and bounced back down. The referee ruled it as a goal, but the argument about whether it crossed the goal line or not has raged ever since. Since that victory, England hadn't won any championships, making this final even more meaningful.

In the world of English women's football, Germany were our biggest rivals. They'd defeated us in three previous championships, leaving us keen to redress the balance. The final was scheduled to take place at Wembley Stadium, with an enthusiastic crowd of 87,000 fans eagerly awaiting the match. Naturally, the players felt the pressure, but we'd learned to embrace that tension and use it to drive us on. We approached the final with the mindset that it was just another game. Personally, I've always stayed calm in high-stakes moments, and interestingly enough this has seemed to rub off on the players. The Lionesses had complete confidence in our carefully crafted game plan for this significant showdown.

Jill Scott, Lionesses midfielder

On match days Sarina would be brimming with confidence because her preparation work was already done. If the opposing team made changes to their line-up she would make a note of it on the tactics sheet for everyone to see. but she would only have a one-on-one conversation with a few players if they were directly going up against the changed opponent.

On the day of the Euro 2022 final something happened during the warm-up. Germany's star player, Alexandra Popp, had to leave the pitch. In the semi-finals she had singlehandedly knocked out France with two goals. Sarina calmly entered the dressing room and told us that Popp wouldn't be playing. She then let Leah Williamson and Millie Bright know that they'd be facing a different player, and explained how they might need to adjust their approach now that Popp was out. Sarina remained calm and composed, and she showed no emotion. Her presence helped us tremendously on the day on which we were about to write ourselves into the history books.

It was a quiet morning before we headed to Wembley on the coach, but the journey was something else. When we left the hotel and boarded the coach we could hear two helicopters flying overhead, broadcasting live. The entire route was lined with supporters on foot or in their cars, cheering us on. Everyone on the bus had goose-bumps. We knew it could be a special day and that we'd unleashed a wave of excitement across the country in the last few weeks.

There were also German supporters in attendance. But when we stepped out onto the pitch for the first time and heard tens of thousands of fans cheering us, it was unforgettable.

After the warm-up we returned to the dressing room. The final was starting in just five minutes, and the team knew what they needed to do. I addressed the players, emphasising that it was a day for everyone to enjoy. This was the game we'd all been waiting for, for which we had given our all, each and every day. Once again, we should commit ourselves to playing our very best football. For ourselves, for our team, our loved ones and our fans.

A little later, the players stood waiting in the tunnel. I witnessed the bond of understanding between them, and the place was buzzing with a belief that they would accomplish their mission. The collective energy of the team was magnificent to see. They were ready.

Leah Williamson, Lionesses defender (captain in Euro 2022)

Playing the final against Germany at Wembley was a dream come true for us. It was something we'd longed for, but we knew it came with immense pressure. A crowd of 87,000 would be cheering us on, making it a game of huge proportions. We'd faced pressure in the tournament before, like in the opening game and the quarter-final against Spain, and had come out on top. But this was different. This was the final against Germany and the pressure was on a whole different level.

I exchanged a glance with Sarina during our last tactical meeting, just hours before the final began. It gave me a sense of confidence to know that she'd been in a similar position several times before. She understood the situation and knew how to get us ready for the final. Her message to us was simple yet powerful: we didn't have to do anything. These words resonated with us, reminding us that we didn't need to feel burdened by the expectations or the need to win. They gave us a sense of freedom and the ability to just focus on playing our game.

We knew we didn't have to win the game, but winning was all we wanted, our greatest desire. Despite this, Sarina's message gave us a sense of calm. We'd prepared for the final, and I personally felt a huge responsibility to the team and all the supporters who'd waited for this moment. I had an emotional connection with them and wanted to give it my all. Sarina's words made me understand that I should enjoy the game by focusing on what I loved doing – playing football. Pressure was a privilege, and we'd earned the opportunity to play in the final. This thought was empowering, and it gave us an extra boost to go out there and do what we do best.

On the day of the final it felt like everything was going wrong. The curtains in our hotel room were faulty and kept opening and closing throughout the night. It was nearly impossible to get a good night's sleep with that distraction. But each time Sarina, always composed, reassured us that others would handle these problems. She encouraged us to stay focused on the game. Her calmness and confidence helped put us at ease. Despite the challenges, we were able to maintain our concentration and stay mentally prepared for the final.

Sarina's message to us was direct – *stick to the plan*. We'd prepared well for this game and knew how to beat Germany. We'd trained for all possible scenarios, and if we stuck to our game plan, had a great chance of making history and changing people's lives.

This was our chance to make our dream come true – the one we'd held close to our hearts for so long. The moment had finally arrived, and we were ready to step onto the pitch and fight for our goal. It was time to give it our all and make our dream a reality.

As we stood in the players' tunnel, waiting to step onto the pitch for the final, Sarina was giving out high fives to everyone. It was a moment of excitement and anticipation. I couldn't help but smile because I knew this was it – the moment of truth. I was fired up, ready to give it my all and make our dream a reality. The thought of playing in the final and getting the chance to make history was magical. It was a feeling I'll never forget.

THE DEFINING MOMENT

It was amazing to see the players emerge from the tunnel. The home fans cheered them on, transforming their nerves into positive energy. I saw that they were beaming with pride, knowing how hard they had worked to get to this moment. As a member of the staff, I felt calm because we'd prepared well for this game. It was now up to our players to execute our game plan.

Germany and England were evenly matched, and both teams had chances to score. But Mary Earps, our goalkeeper, made some fantastic saves, and the game remained goalless. Then, in the 62nd minute Ella Toone was on the end of a long through ball and finished off in phenomenal style by lobbing the ball over the German keeper. It was 1–0 to England.

But Germany weren't giving up. Lina Magull was a big threat, and she hit the crossbar before finally scoring in the 79th minute. The score was level, and the game went into extra-time.

The magic moment we were all waiting for came in the 110th minute. Chloe Kelly scored after a corner kick, and Wembley Stadium erupted in cheers. It was 2–1 to England, and we knew we'd won.

The final whistle blew and the game was over. We'd beaten Germany in extra-time and become European champions. As I turned to my team, the realisation sank in – we'd done it! I cheered and what followed was a group hug. It was an incredible performance, not just from the players but also from the staff. I was filled with happiness, but also a sense of calm. At that moment, I didn't fully grasp the magnitude of what we'd achieved and how it would impact on the people of England.

I walked onto the pitch to thank the referee for her role in the game. Without thinking, I kissed the bracelet on my right wrist. It was a meaningful gesture for me and my sister Diana. She had told me to seize this prize, and I had just done so. I was still calm, not emotional. The only thing I felt was a deep connection with my sister. She always supported me, attending every game no matter where we played. She was more than just a sister – she was my companion and my best friend. I shared everything with her. As a coach, you pray for the good health of everyone around you, but you have no control over it. It was incredibly tough for me when I found out that Diana was seriously ill. I tried my best to be there for her, but I also had responsibilities in England for the games, the training camps and the European Championship. She would have loved to witness our triumph, but it wasn't meant to be.

There was one match with the Lionesses that Diana was able to attend. It was an away game against Luxembourg, and she drove herself down there to support us. The highlight of that trip was the journey back home. It was a special moment with my father, my brother Tom, Diana and myself all in the car. It was a cherished moment for our family.

As the situation worsened, I gathered my staff together and had a difficult conversation about the possibility of me being absent on the day Diana passed away. It was a challenging discussion, but I was amazed by their understanding and support. They wished me well for the time I had left with Diana, and their reaction truly touched me. It was crucial for me to ensure that preparations continued with minimal disruption, so we discussed potential changes in roles and responsibilities among the staff in case I had to leave. This discussion deepened our bond, and provided me with a sense of calm and freedom during such a difficult and sad time.

Sadly, what had been inevitable arrived much sooner than expected. Diana's health was not improving, and she had just a few weeks left to live. It was the end of April. I wanted to be by her side, so I reached out to Mark Bullingham, the CEO of the FA, and shared the heartbreaking situation with him. Before I could ask if I could be with Diana, he immediately responded with compassion, saying, 'Stay in the Netherlands so you can be with your sister. That's the most important thing in your life right now.'

I'd have completely understood if Mark had also enquired about the impact on the Lionesses or expected me to be in England to handle everything. After all, he'd appointed me with the goal of leading the team to become European champions. But he never did ask those questions. All I felt was his unwavering support, and I treasured it immensely.

During Diana's final weeks I was able to be with her again. At a certain point she told me that I had to go back to the training camp with the Lionesses. I was scared that she might pass away unexpectedly without me at her side. I asked if I could wear her bracelet, so I could always have a piece of her with me, even when I was in England. We'd talked about getting matching tattoos, but unfortunately we never got the chance. After the Euros, I decided

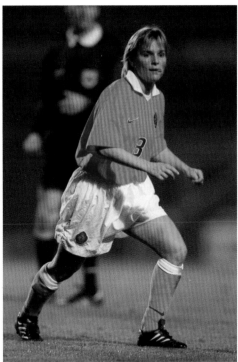

Aged 6 I joined a football team and fearlessly played alongside the boys.

I'm wearing the famous orange jersey as the Netherlands take on England in a World Cup qualifier, October 1997.

Dutch supporters surround the national team bus during Euro 2017.

Victory is sealed in Euro 2017, with Leeuwinnen players
and staff celebrating the moment.

The Leeuwinnen roaring in celebration as they lift the Euro 2017
trophy after their victory in the thrilling final against Denmark.

We all proudly meet King Willem-Alexander at a royal
gathering, showcasing the 2017 trophy.

On the barge with the Leeuwinnen at the victory
parade in Utrecht, 2017.

The Leeuwinnen's full-time huddle at the 2019 World Cup.

Grateful for the fans' support – I acknowledge the crowd after
the World Cup final defeat against the United States in 2019. It was
a disappointing loss – not just for me, but for the entire team.

Heartbreak in Yokohama – I console Vivianne Miedema following our penalty shoot-out loss against the United States in the quarter-final of the Tokyo Olympic Games, July 2021.

Standing beside my statue at the KNVB campus after its unveiling, June 2021.

I address the Lionesses during a huddle at a friendly against Switzerland in Zurich's Stadion Letzigrund, June 2022.

Ella Toone wheels away in celebration following her crucial goal
in the Euro 2022 quarter-final against Spain in Brighton.

Arjan Veurink and I celebrate
the victory against Spain,
Euro 2022.

A special tribute – I kiss my bracelet
in honour of my sister Diana after
the final whistle.

Record-breaking attendance – the screen at Wembley Stadium displays 87,192, the biggest ever crowd at a women's game in the Euros, during the Euro 2022 final between England and Germany.

Royal congratulations – I was honoured to receive my medal from the Prince of Wales, as President of the FA, after England beat Germany.

The Lionesses celebrate their victory at the trophy ceremony.

United as one – the England team huddle together
after losing the 2023 World Cup final.

Pure joy – Ella Toone and teammates
celebrate her opening goal against
Australia in the 2023 World Cup
semi-final in Sydney.

At the World Cup 2023.

to get the tattoo on the inside of my wrist of the same image that was on her bereavement card. It was a way to feel a connection with her.

Exactly one week after leaving the training camp at St George's Park to be with Diana, I returned for a friendly match against Belgium. I was moved by the support everyone gave me during this difficult time. The players and staff were incredible, and our two 'captains' even asked if it was OK to wear black armbands as a sign of support. It reminded me how close we were as a team, and I know that Diana would have been proud of me.

Of course, it was an emotional experience for me. Thankfully, the team's sports psychologist was always there for support, and there were moments when I could talk to her about my grief. I tried my best to put my sadness aside during that period. I thought a lot about Diana and found a way of honouring her during the Euros. I did breathing exercises and rearranged my room so that I could play music and light a candle for her every day.

Considering the circumstances, I was doing pretty well, all things considered. But, deep down, I still felt the emotions, you know? The morning before the big final, all of a sudden, I got really emotional. I couldn't let that happen. I was scared it would overwhelm me during the match, and that was the last thing I wanted. I knew I could let my emotions out after the final, but not before. The final was such an intense experience, and I couldn't let my emotions get in the way. That's why I made a point to talk to the psychologist the day before the game. I needed to release all of my emotions that day, and it made a huge difference.

So when I gave a little kiss to the bracelet on my wrist I was saying, 'We did it, Diana, we're European champions!' These intense moments bring the team even closer together. They're just a part of life. When you spend so much time together, you end up sharing these moments. Some of the players have gone through similar experiences, and now they come to me to talk about them.

Beth Mead, Lionesses forward

During Euro 2022 Sarina had a remarkable intuition for knowing when to reach out to a player. It was like she could sense it. Sarina and I had this special bond because we both had seriously ill family members – her sister and my mother. Going through something so devastating brought us closer together, as we understood each other's struggles on a deep level. We showed a different kind of care towards each other.

I'll always remember how Sarina supported me when my mother passed away. She gave me the space to mourn and offered her shoulder to lean on whenever I needed it. She genuinely wanted to be there for me as a person, and it made a tremendous difference.

The death of my sister and how our team handled it had a big impact on the staff at work. It reminded us that life isn't always easy and pleasant; tough things happen too. It was important for me to open up and let others know I was struggling. It showed that it's OK for anyone to take time off when they need to deal with real-life issues. In a team of dedicated professionals, this was an important message to send. Normally, we don't share personal problems when we go on training camps. Staff members usually deal with them on their own, even if it affects their personal lives. But recently, we started sharing these kinds of things earlier, so that we can find solutions together when someone needs support at home.

When I looked up after kissing my bracelet, I couldn't believe my eyes. Tens of thousands of fans were in delirium. The players remained on the pitch, euphoric, long after the final whistle before they went back down the tunnel. The press conference had already started when the players burst into the room, dancing with excitement. I couldn't hold back my smile. The room was dark, and the bright lights of the cameras made it difficult to see what was happening properly. In her excitement, goalkeeper Mary Earps walked straight towards me and stood on a chair, thinking it was the press conference table. But it was actually a flimsy plank, definitely not meant for standing on. I looked at Mary and mouthed the words 'No, no!' I tried to grab her hand and in that split second wondered if the plank would actually support her weight. But Mary didn't stop, and before I knew it she was dancing on the plank. Celebrating a moment like this was simply awesome. Fortunately, Mary got down unscathed and the press conference continued.

David Gerty, head of women's football communications

Sarina understands the significance of communicating with the media to promote women's football. She believes it's crucial to strengthen the bond with fans and to show more people the sport's true values. The right message can have the power to encourage women to become more involved in the community and create greater opportunities for themselves. Together with the players, this is the story she wants to share.

Unlike some coaches, who view communication as just another part of the job, Sarina places great importance on it. She sees it as a vital aspect of her role and takes the time to lay a solid foundation for effective communication. She believes in proper preparation and involving others in the process. That's why we spend a lot of time with her, working on the message effectively.

One of our most important messages centres around achieving equal rights for women in sports and removing barriers that restrict girls and women from participating in football. On the back of the performances and visibility of the Lionesses, we've created a platform at the Football Association (FA) that allows players and staff to share their message and values with the outside world.

In the lead-up to Euro 2022 it became evident that changes in the government's education policy were necessary to enhance these opportunities. Many schoolgirls in England were receiving the message that opportunities for them did not exist in football. Our players were well aware of this, as many had experienced it first hand. Or they constantly heard the same story from their loved ones, families and friends. Girls were encouraged to pursue other activities. Conversely, boys at school were encouraged to play football and take full advantage of the available facilities.

Both during and after Euro 2022 we used the platform to speak out and push for change. Immediately following the victory celebrations in Trafalgar Square, the players discussed with each other the legacy we wanted to leave for the wider community. Despite being exhausted from the intense tournament and the overwhelming celebrations, the players didn't talk about holiday plans. Instead they were driven to advocate for more change after this major success. The letter we wrote about equal rights for women was not just any message from the Lionesses. We dedicated a lot of time to discussing it – as well as speaking to experts to find ways to break down barriers and make a difference – and the players were and still are fully committed to facilitating this.

I endorse the importance of this message unconditionally. What the team has accomplished is extremely powerful and moving. They have brought about a positive change in society, first through their magnificent performances, and second by pinpointing a societal problem and coming up with solutions themselves. They also undertook action with the FA in the year after their success in the Euros so that something actually happens. This all makes me additionally proud of this team.

Our communication strategy focuses on the impact we can have by being successful. The platform is ready, the message is prepared and the players are able to use it, but only success can break barriers in society. Thanks to the success of the Lionesses, we secured significant media attention, especially in the latter stages of the competition. The attention we gained was also due to the passionate message the players shared about equal rights. As a former PE teacher, I know how crucial sports are in schools, so I also provide guidance on one of the measures that can bring about changes in governance. It's a practical change that has been embraced by the prime minister and is being implemented throughout England. To me, this is the true success of the Lionesses.

That evening we threw a party in the hotel for our family and friends. It was wonderful to have the players and staff reunited with their loved ones after the enforced separation because of Covid-19. I had a great time at the party, trying to talk to as many people as possible. Without our friends and family, many of the players wouldn't have had the opportunity to play in the final. Their support over the years has been tremendous, and it's fantastic to celebrate with them. The pride was evident, and we all shared the feeling that we had achieved something special together.

Millie Bright, Lionesses defender (captain)

As soon as the final whistle blew, my emotions exploded. I ran straight to Leah Williamson. Before the tournament we made a pact to stick together and give it our all until the end. Before the final she wrote me a note, and that meant a lot to me. I gave her a big hug and we looked at each other. We did it, we finally cracked it!

Those were the longest five minutes of my life. I wish the elation we felt on the pitch could last forever. My emotions were raw, and I wanted to hug all the fans.

The most challenging part of the tournament still lay ahead. I didn't see it coming. After all the celebrations were over, everyone went home. I felt a sense of sadness. We'd been together for so long, and now that intense period was behind us. Why was it so quiet here? Where was everyone? What am I doing here? What should I do now?

I had to adjust to going back to my normal life. But life outside the bubble brought something amazing as we hadn't realised the impact we'd made. It was only now that I truly understood the significance of it all. Seeing the flags in the streets where I lived and the posters of us celebrating with the trophy at Wembley, I felt the love from our supporters who'd been with us all along. We didn't just win a tournament, we ignited the entire country. We'd changed women's sports and women's football. The world was different after the finals, and the feeling overwhelmed me.

7

CHALLENGES ON THE WAY TO DOWN UNDER

In April 2023, in preparation for the World Cup that summer, we played a friendly game against Australia, who were co-hosting the tournament with New Zealand. I wasn't concerned about what others were saying at that time, like the fact that we'd won 30 games in a row since I'd become coach of the Lionesses. It was obviously a great statistic, but my team and I were more focused on improving our game in preparation for the World Cup. Of course, we wanted to play well and win every game, but the most important thing was being ready for the tournament that summer.

Losing 2–0 to Australia in the friendly gave us valuable insights for the World Cup. Our initial response was that we'd played way below our best level, and straight after the game we looked into why we'd played so badly. We knew that we'd lost the ball in possession too often, that our gameplay was too hectic and inaccurate, and that we'd made too many costly individual mistakes.

The information the analysis had given us was valuable. We'd already experienced a similar situation in a match against the Czech Republic, where our opponents had adopted a highly defensive strategy by forming a compact block at the back. If we made a mistake in possession in their half, they'd swiftly counterattack and pose a serious threat. Australia used exactly the same tactics, capitalising on our errors when on the ball. Such scenarios were bound to arise in the World Cup, which reinforced our primary focus on maintaining possession in crucial moments and avoiding unnecessary turnovers. On other occasions we planned to take calculated risks, accelerate the pace, surprise the opposition and inject more dynamism into our play. We also knew that we had to conduct a deeper analysis of our opponents' potential tactics.

Another observation was that the timing of the Australia match might actually have been beneficial, as strange as this may sound, as it was probably a very good thing for the team to experience a defeat three months before the start of the World Cup. After every game we analyse what's gone well and what needs improvement, and this loss suddenly brought a sense of urgency to our camp.

We'd already talked about a couple of areas for improvement in previous evaluations: making better choices on the ball, and being more secure on the ball at those moments when there was more space between players and no transition was expected. But if these shortcomings in our play weren't punished, the message was less effective. Against Australia that self-evidently wasn't the case – and we'd been punished.

So we gratefully took advantage of the situation: this could happen. Everyone now felt the need to do better, to find solutions together, to hold onto the ball or swiftly launch a counterattack, although we didn't have the opportunity to share our insights straight after the match. The players scattered back to their respective clubs, which were now entering the decisive phase of their competitions, both domestic and European. It would be a nice starting point for the first training camp after the lost match.

CONFIDENCE THROUGH ONGOING LEARNING

All the players have their own plans to help them get better at the game. During our training camps, time and attention are spent on this at the end of sessions. In the afternoon we have one-on-one meetings with the staff.

These meetings are always set up beforehand, so we know who we'll be talking to.

In many of these meetings, we watch video clips of games played by the Lionesses, as well as their own club games. These games contain lots of interesting moments that are worth discussing. We focus on as many as 10 to 12 clips in each meeting, watching them to see what we expect from a Lionesses player. Each player brings their own skills to the game, and it's these skills that we want to improve and make the most of. Together with the staff, we make it clear what we want to see from the players.

For instance, there's this one winger who doesn't always try to beat her opponent in order to get past her. We found some video clips that showed her either passing the ball back or trying to dribble around her opponent and then getting tackled and losing the ball. So I asked her why she chose to pass instead of taking on her opponent. I told her it didn't matter if she lost the ball. In fact, I encouraged her to do it again. We give her permission to make mistakes.

Lucy Bronze, Lionesses defender

Sarina and I have a different opinion when it comes to handling pressure. We've both achieved a lot in our careers. Sarina believes in downplaying the conversation about winning the tournament to take the pressure off the team. In one interview I emphasised the importance of winning, but Sarina reminded me that it's not all about winning. I understood that she was trying to ease the pressure on the less experienced players, although there are also experienced players who thrive under this pressure and need it to perform at their best.

Managing a group of 23 to 30 players successfully is no easy feat, especially when considering how to handle pressure. It's also important not to underestimate the pressure that Sarina was under herself when leading the Lionesses. Maybe her way of coping was to downplay our chances of winning Euro 2022. Unfortunately, the media are quick to pick up on this and increase the pressure on us. The approach we take depends on the experience level of the players. For example, with a more experienced group I think it's important to emphasise that our main objective is winning. We've been playing in tournaments for many years, making it as far as the quarter- or semi-finals, so it's precisely that pressure we need to push ourselves to go one more step and win the final.

The pressure leading up to the 2023 World Cup didn't feel any different. Winning Euro 2022 was the ultimate goal for us after years of disappointment [of getting knocked out]. That victory gave us the confidence and belief that we needed to succeed in the World Cup. We knew that the greater the pressure, the better we played against the best teams in Europe, and even in the world. Our experience helped us remain calm and composed under pressure. If a team can maintain the same level of performance under pressure as they do in other circumstances, then they'll achieve good results.

Sarina led by example during games, remaining calm and focused. She always had a plan in place and executed it calmly and convincingly when needed. Pressure had no effect on her, and she stuck to the tactics she'd prepared. That was also her message to us: keep performing your tasks under pressure.

PEOPLE-MANAGEMENT STRATEGIES FOR A STRONGER TEAM

While preparing for the 2023 World Cup in Australia and New Zealand we faced a number of setbacks due to some of our players suffering long-term injuries, a consequence of the incredible growth of women's football and the speed at which it's now played. This requires attention, lots of attention, and action.

The coaching staff must take appropriate action when a player has to pull out of a major tournament. When I first hear of a severe injury to one of our players, my first thought is about the individual. Her World Cup or Euro dreams have been crushed by unexpected misfortune. All her investment in elite sport, all the sacrifices. I understand how painful and upsetting that is, having experienced it myself. So I try to contact the player as soon as possible and comfort her as best as I can.

Maintaining a personal connection with players is crucial to me. I keep in touch with them throughout their recovery process. We communicate through phone calls, messages and visits during their club games, all in addition to their contact with the medical staff regarding their rehabilitation progress and predicted date when they can play again.

After my initial contact with the player I take some time to process my own disappointment. A player's absence affects not only the player herself but the whole squad as well. Once I've come to terms with it, I start thinking of solutions. Instead of dwelling on what has happened, I focus on the options we have among the available players.

Every Tuesday we discuss the performance of England players in domestic competitions and analyse which positions would be the best fit for an individual player. We also consider the available options if our first-choice player drops out for any reason.

In the lead-up to the 2023 World Cup, we lost three key players: Beth Mead in November, Fran Kirby in

February and Leah Williamson in April. They were all crucial members of the team during Euro 2022, with Leah as the captain. By doubling up on positions during our analyses, we were able to quickly switch to another option in the event of an injury. We adopt this approach throughout the training process and tournament, working on fine-tuning our style of play.

Lucy Bronze, Lionesses defender

As we prepared for the 2023 World Cup, the team discussed the importance of experienced players like myself. I'd already been considered one of the more experienced players during the 2019 World Cup, and during that tournament I tried to go above and beyond to support the less experienced players on the team. I quickly learned that it took a lot out of me both physically and mentally. By the time we reached the semi-finals I was exhausted. That's when I realised it was important for me to stay true to myself and use my experience on the pitch. The younger players could rely on me to guide them, and this approach was more effective and less draining. By conserving my energy in this way, I was able to make a bigger impact on the game.

During our preparations, we had a discussion with Sarina about the World Cup and how it differed from the Euros.

The World Cup was a bigger and more challenging tournament in many ways, and all the players needed to mentally gear themselves up for it. This was particularly important for us since we'd recently achieved success in Euro 2022. That tournament was played in our own country, so we felt more at home and comfortable. Our families were nearby, and we could easily stay in touch with them. We knew the stadiums and their surroundings well, and we could predict how long it would take to get there. When we took a walk before a game we didn't have to adjust to a new environment. This allowed us to focus more on the game ahead.

Now, however, we were facing the challenge of playing the World Cup on the other side of the world. While English is spoken in Australia and New Zealand, it was still a different continent for us. The biggest change was the vast distances and the time-zone differences, which meant that staying in touch with our families would be much more difficult. Since this contact was crucial for helping us relax, we knew we'd have to put in extra effort. Travelling between host cities was also more demanding due to the longer distances.

On the pitch things were very different from the Euros as well. In Europe we were familiar with most of the teams and their distinctive playing styles, albeit with European influences. However, at the World Cup, teams from different continents come together, including teams that we were less familiar with and whose playing styles differed from those in Europe. This is what makes the World Cup special, but it also had a greater impact than the Euros. It was important for us to recognise this, so that I could use my experience to make a positive impact specifically in this tournament.

In my opinion, the World Cup finals are the most enjoyable tournaments to participate in on and off the pitch. Nowadays, I've learned to share my experience with my teammates, especially during the tournament, by simply being myself and communicating with them effectively on the pitch. I don't need to change who I am to make an impact. By establishing and strengthening my connections with others through my experience and skills, I can contribute significantly to the team's success. Sarina encouraged me to do just that, and it has had a positive effect.

CONGESTED FIXTURE LISTS FOR THE PLAYERS

Before we headed out to Australia, we faced a new problem: this was a key moment in our preparations, but the players' schedules were jam-packed, and there didn't seem to be an easy solution.

It's fantastic that women's football is coming on in leaps and bounds. But that comes with its challenges too. First of all, it's essential for all parties – FIFA, UEFA, the respective Football Associations, clubs, players and coaches – to enter into and stay in dialogue with each other. The number of games, in combination with day-to-day routines, fixture lists, facilities for players, periods of rest and lifestyle coaching are subjects that must be discussed to help develop the sport on an ongoing basis. All of this must also take into account the health of the players.

The most important thing is that players and coaches are part of the discussion. It's critical to involve players and coaches to avoid talking over their heads. The players' union, FIFPro, has an important role to play in finding a solution. The challenge is to coordinate all national and continental games, and arrange events like the World Cup in such a way that players can get enough rest, especially after a major tournament. It's essential to make this happen before the 2027 World Cup so that we can count on all of the top players being available.

For the World Cup in Australia and New Zealand, we still hadn't resolved that problem. Clubs continued to send a message by not releasing players on time for the preparations, but I couldn't accept this as it put the players at a disadvantage, especially at such a crucial time. It took a lot of effort and persuasion on the part of myself and a number of colleagues to convince the clubs otherwise, but we knew what we were fighting for.

Our expertise and scientific studies have shown that if a player has a two-week rest period, they need to resume training to perform at their best during the World Cup. By not releasing players for the national side, players would have to seek out individual solutions to train outside the club and the national team, without access to our expertise and training facilities, meaning there would be no overview or control of their workload. Our well-prepared programme, accompanied by our supportive staff and top-notch facilities, significantly increases this overview and control.

Luckily, the clubs have started recognising the importance of the players' needs, and we were able to begin our programme and preparations on schedule. We drew a number of lessons from this and will soon be entering into a dialogue with the clubs about how we can improve things together in the future, in the interests of the players, the clubs and the England national team. But fortunately, we were in a position to prepare the players physically and mentally for the World Cup in Australia and New Zealand.

PART TWO

A NEW GENERATION

8

IMPACT ON WOMEN

EFFECT ON WOMEN

I sometimes imagine myself as a teenager in today's world. I'd be in the stands wearing a shirt with the name of my favourite player, like Miedema, Martens, White or Mead. I'd dream about playing in front of a huge crowd in a few years' time. Maybe I'd be part of ADO Den Haag's first team and training five days a week, as that's what professional clubs in the Netherlands do nowadays.

In another scenario, I'd be in the stands analysing the team tactics of the Leeuwinnen or the Lionesses. How will the players execute the coach's tactical plan? How much do they desire to win?

The promotion of equal opportunities for everyone in sport is something I hold dear. This goes beyond simply improving opportunities for women and girls in football, as is highlighted by this book. I strongly believe in the power of diversity and inclusion in teams. That is why I will be committing myself fully to creating an environment in which all top athletes and staff have the same opportunities, regardless of their background, culture, gender identity, sexual preference and religion.

I know that this is shared by my players and the FA who are doing a lot of important work to make sure more girls have access not only to the England pathway, but the game as a whole. A big restructure to the talent pathway is already helping more young girls from all backgrounds to find a place to play and also ensuring that the very best talent can be identified. The players' and the FA's determination to provide every girl with the chance to play in school has inclusivity at the heart of the message and I hope will also have a transformational impact on society. Of course, there's always more we can all do and it's a challenge we are all committed to.

WHAT YOU SEE, YOU CAN BECOME

'What you see, you can become, but what you can't see, you can't become.' When I was young I had my hair cut short so that I could play football. Back then, football was seen as a sport for boys, and many girls weren't allowed to play by their parents. They gave up, even though football was what many girls loved the most. I was so passionate about the game that I played anyway. I was fortunate to have open-minded parents who believed that it was important for their children to pursue what made them happy. And for me, that was playing football.

Of course, the boys on my team were aware that I was a girl, but it never bothered me. They knew I could play well, and that was all that mattered. Most of the opposing teams didn't even realise I was a girl, and I was fine with that. Sometimes they'd find out – usually when a parent on the sidelines was upset about us winning – and in those moments, derogatory remarks would be directed at me. But I always tried my best to brush it off and not let it affect me.

During my time in primary school I didn't have any idols or role models. While I'd often say that I wanted to become a PE teacher when I grew up, because I knew that was a possibility, I never expressed my desire to become a football coach. It simply wasn't seen as a feasible option for women. Even just playing football was frowned upon.

For all the teenagers in the stands today, I hope that they are given the opportunities they yearn for – whether that be as players or as coaches.

Lieke Martens, Leeuwinnen forward

When I was young it was unusual for girls to play football. Being on the football pitch meant being surrounded by boys, and people would always comment when they saw a girl playing. There were a lot of stereotypes about girls who played football: that they were all lesbians with short hair. But that wasn't me. I always had long hair and would talk with my friends about cute boys. Yes, I wore a lot of tracksuits, but that was because I was always playing football. But I also enjoyed dressing up in dresses and high heels. That confused a lot of people because it didn't fit their stereotypes.

I thought about this a lot during my early teenage years. I felt like I was being pigeonholed. Was I really that masculine? Was I the person others thought I was? It motivated me to embrace being a woman who played football. I had friends who played hockey and others who played football, and that was okay. We were all just different in the sports we enjoyed. We were able to get along on and off the pitch.

Fortunately, there's been a real change in how female football players are seen, and I'm proud to have played a role in that simply by being myself. Now, any woman can play football, no matter who they are.

I have regular conversations with Lucy Bronze about the impact that the Lionesses have on girls and women in England. These discussions are important because we have some shared experiences and also some differences. Lucy, like me, had to cut her hair to continue playing football, but in her case it was her brother who did it. She used to play with boys until the FA decided to ban girls from playing with them, citing safety concerns.

However, Lucy's experience playing with boys was positive. They didn't see any difference between boys and girls, and she was just another friend who happened to be good at football. This gave her a lot of confidence and respect. Unfortunately, she was no longer allowed to play with them.

Thankfully, Lucy had supportive parents who'd take her to training sessions an hour and a half away, even though these took place only twice a week and she wanted to play every day. The lack of a girls' team in her area made it even more challenging for her to pursue her passion for football, but this has fuelled her drive to fight for better opportunities for girls and women in the sport.

It hasn't been an easy journey for her. I tease her by calling her the oldest player in the squad but she's actually from a different generation to me, even though she's the nearest in age to me. Her generation realised earlier than mine that they had to stand up and fight for better opportunities for women. Lucy understands that it's easier for players than coaches to get positive publicity. A good performance in a match can bring immediate attention to a player, but for coaches it usually takes a series of good results or an exceptional performance in a tournament.

What Lucy Bronze and I both have in common is a sense of responsibility to create better opportunities for girls and women, both within and beyond the world of football. Interestingly, neither of us initially started out with this goal in mind. Like me, Lucy had an intense passion for the sport and was fiercely competitive. In the past it was all about winning games on the playground, but now it's about competing in the World Cup. It was only later in life that we felt this responsibility to make a difference for others, which was accompanied by a feeling of unease because it was unfamiliar territory. Despite that, it became something we strongly believed in and stood for.

For Lucy, her primary focus is on improving opportunities for women in England, although she recognises that the impact of this goes way beyond England. English football often receives significant attention worldwide, and as a result the Lionesses have become role models for girls and women across the globe. If we succeed in enhancing opportunities here, it will have a ripple effect internationally.

During our conversations we reached an important conclusion: success drives change. The impact which we want to achieve with the Lionesses has been under way for longer than since 2022. Lucy has been advocating for better opportunities in women's football for many years, and progress has already been made. But to make even bigger strides and achieve a significant breakthrough, we need success. That's what sets the present apart from the past.

By winning Euro 2022, we gained the momentum to make that breakthrough. The entire country was watching and celebrating our victory in the final. We used that moment as a platform to share our story. It reached the royal family, politicians, professional and amateur clubs, and millions of enthusiastic people who wanted to join us in making this change happen. Without this victory we may have made progress, but not the breakthrough we achieved.

And we can't simply stop here. We have to keep taking steps forward, embracing the drive to keep winning. To achieve this, we must forge our own path. We can learn lessons from men's football and ensure that the positive aspects from the men's game are reflected in women's football. In England, the successes of 2022 and 2023 have provided us with a platform to improve opportunities. Young girls like Lucy no longer have to travel long distances to train. They can play football with boys from a young age because it meets their needs, and benefits both girls and boys. Every time girls see women who have reached the highest level in the sport, it inspires them and shows them what's possible. More and more women are excelling as players, coaches and referees, making women in these roles increasingly normal. But we still have work to do. Our goal is to open doors for girls and women who share a passion for the game.

My responsibility for speaking out more often has grown over the years. And as Lucy often says, 'Success drives change. Even if you're not always in the spotlight, your presence matters.'

TWENTY YEARS

If we don't do anything extra, I think it'll take another 20 years before women get the same respect as men in football. I'm proud of the progress made with the Leeuwinnen and Lionesses in the past years, but 20 years is a long wait. Honestly, even a year is too much.

I'm not just talking about women's football, but also about appreciating the skills and talent that women bring to men's football. Women are valuable in many jobs, and other industries are already benefiting from this. However, the football world is stuck in its ways.

If we do something extra, we can quicken this process. I truly believe that pushing harder can make it happen in five years, indeed the faster the better. I compare it to a game where we're losing 4–2. Not 2–0, because there has already been some progress. We'll emerge victorious when the score is level at 4–4, when things are balanced again. When you're 4–2 down you go in search of goals, take more risks and go on the attack more. That's what we need to do now.

I often hear that we need to do more work. This is exactly true. We need to distinguish between 'the recognition of women's football' and 'more women in the football industry'. Both are important, and both need support. If we manage to score one of these two goals, the score would be a loss at 4–3 instead of a draw at 4–4. Unfortunately, we would still suffer a loss.

It all begins with a strong desire and appreciation for women's football. Both the FA and the KNVB are making progress, which is a positive sign. While I've been away from the KNVB for a while now, what I've noticed at the FA is that it's not just about changing the structure. It's also about how men and women interact and communicate. From day one at the FA, the communication has taken place on a level playing field and I feel appreciated. Likewise, the facilities I've had access to since my first day at the FA show me that they are committed to achieving equality.

However, more needs to be done. There are still too many obstacles preventing girls and women from having better opportunities in football. Overcoming these challenges requires a multifaceted approach, fostering inclusivity both within and outside of football. It's not about a single specific action, but rather the accumulation of various smaller actions that raise awareness and remove barriers.

Geraint Twose, Lionesses assistant coach

During Euro 2022 the England players and team became widely popular across the country. We didn't fully recognise it at the time because we were focused on the tournament, but after we won we felt the impact of our success. The interest in women's football grew tremendously, with girls and women across the country wanting to play. We were breaking down barriers that had previously kept people from playing.

Our success even had an impact in the rural area of Wales where I grew up. A friend who coached a local club called to tell me that, for the first time, they had established a girls' team. He credited the Lionesses for inspiring this development, which was fantastic to hear.

For me, the final was an incredibly emotional occasion. I hadn't seen my family for the whole of the tournament. Compared with previous tournaments, this time felt different for them because it was being held in England. They were able to watch all the games on TV, so it was almost as if they were right there in the stadium with us. This was true for everyone around me – there was a lot of buzz and excitement surrounding our success.

After winning the final, there was an overwhelming sense of pride. I called my family immediately after the final. I was walking across the pitch at Wembley, and as soon as I heard them, tears welled up in my eyes. It was so emotional and the moment still lingers with me today.

I'm aware of the chance that I have to promote equal opportunities. It's important for our society to achieve this. However, I don't like to be in the spotlight all the time. It can feel uncomfortable because I prefer to put the team in the spotlight. Stepping forward isn't natural for me, but I know that if I do, I will create better opportunities for the next generation.

Here in England they say, 'What you can see, you can be.' It's important to make women visible, women who work at a certain level and set an example for other women, so that young girls can see and know what they can achieve. There are different ways to achieve this. The success with the Leeuwinnen in the Netherlands in recent years has shown girls that they can have opportunities as players or coaches that didn't exist before. We need more campaigns that strengthen this. When women are appointed as the director of a professional football club, and Marianne van Leeuwen is made CEO of the KNVB in the Netherlands, we need to cherish and amplify these achievements for the future.

Lieke Martens, Leeuwinnen forward

The biggest change after winning the Euros with the Leeuwinnen was that many young girls saw what they could achieve. They now had a realistic goal in mind and women to look up to as examples. In 2017 we gave a huge boost to women's football, and as a result the attitude of parents towards the sport changed too. I think many parents would have preferred their daughters to play hockey or volleyball, but we managed to change their mindset. Women's football suddenly became exciting and cool. It was no longer a problem; in fact it was awesome if their daughter played football. I still think that's really fantastic.

With the Leeuwinnen, we aimed to inspire. We were aware of our position as role models. The image we wanted to convey was that of a positive and successful team with approachable players. The connection with the public, which Sarina always emphasised, was so strong that one greatly reinforced the other. It brought us a lot that summer, but it also came with its costs in the years that followed.

I'm not someone who has to be in the spotlight all the time. I quite enjoy being in the background, even within the team. I never felt any different from the other players on the team and I certainly couldn't perform without the other players. However, I noticed that the outside world started focusing more and more on me. This was evident during the tournament, as an increasing amount was being written about me and pressure was put on my shoulders. On the other hand, I was proud of it too. I was a role model for the new generation, and I considered that important enough to accept the drawbacks. I became a well-known figure in the Netherlands, and with that came greater demands and expectations. It became increasingly difficult to remain accessible, especially since I also have a personal life. It changed my life.

First, let's strive for a 25 per cent increase in the number of women working in football organisations. It's crucial that women have more visibility and representation within these structures. This includes not only clubs, but also various committees of the Football Association and other related bodies.

The goal should be to have more women in the boardroom and in decision-making roles. The appointments of Debbie Hewitt and Marianne van Leeuwen as Chair of the FA and CEO of the KNVB respectively have been crucial milestones in football's history. Debbie is the first woman in 157 years of football history in England to lead the FA. The same goes for Marianne: she is the first female CEO of the KNVB in the Netherlands, an organisation that was founded in 1889.

It's just the beginning of where we need to be. There are still too many boardrooms where women aren't in charge. This applies to both professional and amateur football. In amateur football in England and the Netherlands, it's still rare for a woman to hold a position on the board. It's the same in representative bodies of national football associations like the Board of Directors, the Membership Council, the Advisory Board and so on. Women are the exception, and that's no longer acceptable.

Women need to support each other more effectively to bring about this change. What's most important right now is that we encourage each other to develop, but this encouragement comes with certain responsibilities. I've attended professional coaching meetings in the Netherlands on more than one occasion, and I was the only woman there. Increasing the visibility of women coaches at these meetings is critical if we want to achieve our goal of having 25 per cent more women in football organisations.

However, it's not enough to appoint more women to football organisations. We need to change the make-up of the committees that select them. As long as these selection committees are biased towards white men of a certain age, we won't achieve diversity in the footballing world. Fortunately, the Dutch Football Association (KNVB) and the FA have made progress in improving the diversity of its supervisory and advisory boards.

Louis van Gaal, former head coach of the Netherlands men's team

I strongly believe in the potential of women's football. As far back as 2000 I created a comprehensive plan for the Royal Dutch Football Association that emphasised the importance of the women's game. This plan included various key elements that needed to be in place for women's football to thrive. We formed a committee, which included Andries Jonker, the coach of the Leeuwinnen at the time. Within the plan I proposed the idea of having boys and girls play together on the same team.

Women's football has a lot of potential. It is developing faster than men's football, stadiums are filling up and more and more often it's more enjoyable than a men's match. However, it will still take some time before it becomes equal to men's football in many aspects. Physically, women can never catch up, but that doesn't always make the game less attractive. In any case, matches in women's football are less marred by various player protests.

However, I do have concerns about the development of
female coaches. We need to actively support their training
and eliminate any barriers that may exist, so that we can
have more coaches of the calibre of Sarina in the future.

There's a lot that needs to be done. If I had the opportunity to address three challenges in women's football, I'd
focus on improving education and training for girls,
upgrading facilities and ensuring equal financial recognition for top athletes.

The precondition is that investment – both quantitative
and qualitative – has to be made now in women's football. That means investmenting in new facilities and
improving the existing infrastructure. What's more, it's
vital to ensure that the financial means are in place to
support women players in their professional careers.

But we also need to invest in our culture. Culture, of
course, is difficult to change. However, with our current
role models and the attention that has been generated, the
time is ripe to make clear that exactly the same precondi-
tions should exist for boys, girls, men and women.
Football should be for everyone. It should be normal for
girls and women to play and coach football, but unfortunately that's not the case yet. Talented girls and women
should have the same opportunities to grow and develop
as talented boys and men. This investment isn't just about

money, it's about changing attitudes. Just imagine how amazing it would be if the participating countries at the women's World Cup in 2027 have taken the appropriate steps so that they all have a programme up and running with the best facilities under the management of a staff where every expertise is in place and players are optimally prepared.

When it comes to investment, it's clear that women's football is a growing market with incredible potential. This means that now is the perfect time to put money into the women's game. In such a growing market, you can expect extremely high returns with the right choices and investments. Taking this step requires courage, leadership and a vision for the future. Considering the recent successes in the Netherlands, England and now Australia, it's clear that there's no other choice but to make these investments.

9

WINNING WITH THE BEST TEAM

As a coach my primary goal is to develop each player in a way that strengthens the team as a whole, and I pour all my energy into achieving this. But while player development is crucial, sustained success requires more than that. Among other things, it also involves the coaching staff, the relevant football association, the fixture list and myself.

What motivates the players? I want to understand the values they bring with them from home, what stirs them, and how they behave both on and off the pitch. When and why do players form a bond with each other, and when do they not? When does a player take responsibility for herself and the team, and why does another player fail to do so? How do players handle pressure, and what factors contribute to their ability to do so?

I believe it is crucial to know all my players well. All of them. As the head coach of the national team, time is precious, and decisions need to be made. I choose to invest a significant amount of time with my staff and players. Ultimately, in the heat of a game, when pressure is high, you must be able to rely on each other. In my view, you only become a team when you really know each other, when all that is needed is a quick glance to understand a teammate. To observe how a player handles their responsibilities under pressure in a match situation.

We are familiar with the character traits and preferred methods of communication of all our players. It is essential to take these factors into consideration to ensure effective communication. Some players, for instance those who are results driven, respond well to direct and straightforward communication. However, for other players, this type of communication can cause stress, requiring us to adopt a different approach. Our goal is to reach out to all players through effective communication, fostering their development and team bonding. As a coach, decisions always have to be made, such as choosing the coaching methods to be implemented during training sessions. So I strive to understand what motivates each player and determine the most effective approach for their improvement. I adapt my coaching and language accordingly. I reserve harsh criticism only for instances when a player fails to meet expectations, which fortunately seldom occurs. I believe in passionate coaching rather than loud shouting.

Lucy Bronze, Lionesses defender

Sarina is open to hearing other people's opinions as she believes that discussing football situations with players is valuable. However, it's important to base these discussions on accurate information and facts. If you have a reasonable question or suggestion, she's willing to have a conversation about it.

I like being challenging with Sarina. As one of the more experienced players, I often have a different perspective on things. By challenging her, Sarina can improve her coaching performance. She uses the differing opinions as an opportunity for the team to think more creatively about finding solutions during matches.

I value the discussions I have with Sarina, even though sometimes they become lengthy and we don't always agree with each other. I remember one time when we were on a plane after a game, and the pilot announced that we were about to land. At that point we were still engaged in an animated discussion and came to the conclusion that we wouldn't reach a consensus. We decided to agree to disagree, and I was comfortable with that because it showed I could discuss anything directly with Sarina. She never takes things personally.

The staff and I are committed to the development of our players, and we sometimes refer to the 'hard' and 'soft' elements of football. The hard elements encompass the actual game play, while the soft elements focus on bonding, cooperation and leadership. In preparation for major tournaments such as the Euros or the World Cup, we strive to integrate these two elements. For example, if we hold a team talk before a training session at a training camp, we make sure it is football-related. When discussing the opposition, we involve the whole group. Smaller groups tend to concentrate on specific footballing situations related to our style of play, rather than solely focusing on our next opponent. Our team-development sessions are always held in the afternoon or early evening, where we discuss themes such as 'winning behaviours' with the entire team.

Vivianne Miedema, Leeuwinnen, forward

Sarina was always super-organised when she worked with us, the Leeuwinnen. Whenever we stepped onto the training pitch, she had a clear plan in mind. She'd give us a quick explanation of what we were focusing on for the training session and what drills we'd be doing. Later, in our discussions, she'd go over them again. It was straight to the point and made a big impact.

One of Sarina's greatest strengths was that she kept us informed about where we stood as players. It could be tough at times, especially when it seemed like we might not get much playing time. But because Sarina had been successful coaching the Leeuwinnen, we accepted it to some extent. She was amazing at making things clear for us. She built a solid foundation we could always rely on. So far, she's been able to do this for every tournament.

An essential part of developing a team is to create a working space in which everyone can perform at their best. This means ensuring that the players and staff feel safe and supported. We also focus on creating an environment that encourages the team's growth. In competitive sports there's always a lot of rivalry, whether it's within the players' own clubs or in the national team. This competition pushes athletes to give their all and improve their performance. I believe it's crucial for players to focus on their own development and strive to become the best version of themselves. This requires taking action and being willing to make mistakes, because sometimes those mistakes can lead to something amazing. While players have control over their own growth, they don't have control over the coach's decisions on who gets to play. So, taking action and embracing mistakes is important.

Together with my coaching staff, I always try to ensure that they let the players know that they should feel comfortable making mistakes. In fact, we even encourage it in various ways. During team sessions we discuss how making mistakes is a natural part of winning behaviour, and we encourage players to be vulnerable and open to growth as top athletes. On the pitch we dedicate time to practising game situations and offering football solutions based on our principles. We value and support players when they implement these solutions, even if mistakes occur along the way.

IT CAN ALSO BE FUN!

When preparing for a tournament, our team of staff and I put a lot of effort into planning a programme for the players. It's not just about training, but also making sure they have time to relax. And it's not just the players who need that – the staff do too. Working with such talented professionals in all their fields is amazing, but it does require sacrifices. Our staff members are incredibly dedicated and often have to be away from home, especially during tournaments. I believe it's crucial to create an environment where we, as a team, give our all to support the players. We work hard and also enjoy each other's company.

Effort, relaxation, connection. These three things are essential for the growth and well-being of the staff. We believe in working hard and playing together. During training camps, the staff really give it their all, but it's important that they don't burn themselves out completely. To prevent that, we make sure to include moments of relaxation in our programme. Since the staff come from different disciplines, each with their own peak times during the day, we decided to have a group gathering at the end of each training camp day. It's like a daily meeting in the business world, but we add a fun and relaxing activity to it. First, we review the day together, and then we unwind with a drink. It's a time to put away our laptops and have some relaxed conversations, and the team truly values these moments of down time.

When it comes to tournaments, relaxation and unwinding for the staff become even more crucial, as the intensity of the work is even more pronounced. Tournaments last longer and there's something happening every day, especially when we're all together for an extended period. We make an effort to provide the staff with the same important relaxation activities that we offer the players. Family moments, which mean a lot to the players, are equally significant for many staff members, so we make sure to include these in our plans as well. It's important for them to spend time with their loved ones, share experiences, and catch up on how their families and friends are doing, especially because tournaments can have a significant impact on people.

Vivianne Miedema, Leeuwinnen forward

When you're playing in a tournament, one of the most crucial things is having enough time to recover. Of course, that depends on how the games go. For example, in the Euro 2017 final against Denmark we were the team with better fitness because we'd had an easier game in the semi-finals – 3–0 vs England – than the Danes, who'd had to go to extra-time and penalties against Austria. In comparison, during the 2019 World Cup semis, we played 120 minutes against Sweden and had one less day of rest before the final. As a result, there was a noticeable difference in how refreshed we felt when the final kicked off.

Through my experiences in the 2017, 2019 and 2021 tournaments, I realised the importance of seeing my family and friends regularly. Playing a tournament on home turf in 2017 was a huge advantage because my family was nearby, and it was easy to schedule meet-ups with them. Spending time with my family isn't just a distraction; it allows me to be myself completely and provides me with energy. In those moments, I'm not just a football player; I'm someone's daughter or sister.

In the 2019 World Cup, it was more challenging to see my family. Fortunately, they happened to be in France, but not everyone had that opportunity. On the other hand, at the Olympics in Tokyo, due to Covid-19 restrictions, it was strictly forbidden to have any contact with family. The tournament already felt strange with all the empty stadiums, but without my family around it was even more difficult.

I'm grateful to be part of a staff of highly motivated and qualified professionals. It is always hard work, and even harder during the training camps and final tournaments. I don't need to motivate them, as they are highly invested in the team. I feel responsible for the well-being of the entire team, players and staff, where the quality of relaxation is just as important as the quality of effort. It should also be enjoyable.

VISUALISING ALL SCENARIOS

During the England–Spain quarter-final at Euro 2022, we made strategic changes after going 1–0 down. This was not a spur-of-the-moment decision. In modern football, managing substitutions is a crucial process that requires careful planning, insight and execution. Sue Campbell once complimented me on my ability to make effective substitutions, but I remain humble about my skills. Nonetheless, I have strong vision when it comes to making substitutions.

When we did not qualify directly for the 2019 World Cup with the Leeuwinnen, we faced a play-off final against Switzerland to secure a spot in the finals. In the first game in November 2018 we won convincingly with a score of 3–0. For the return game in Switzerland we had prepared for the usual scenarios with the coaching staff.

However, one scenario stuck in my mind that we had not discussed with the rest of the staff. The only situations in which we'd be in trouble against Switzerland was if we received a red card early in the game. What would we do if that happened?

We had an immediate dilemma on our hands. There are certain extreme scenarios that we don't want to plan with everyone, because you don't want this scenario running through people's heads. This was one of those occasions, and I made the decision not to discuss it with the rest of my staff. I worked out a plan for it in my notebook and chose not to share this plan with anyone beforehand.

Louis van Gaal, former head coach of the Netherlands men's team

The most crucial aspect of preparation for a coach leading up to the Euros or World Cup is selecting early on the 23 players you want to take with you. You need to carefully consider the qualities of your players. Once you've got your team ready, it's important to create a plan that answers three key questions: What tactics will you use? What are your strategies if you go behind in the game? And what are your strategies if you go ahead and want to consolidate?

When we were leading in a game and I brought Marten de Roon on, every player understood their role on the pitch: stay compact and see the game out. I'd communicated that beforehand, and everyone knew what their role would be in this scenario. That way it was all clear and each player felt valued because they knew they were making a contribution to the team.

It pleases me to see that Sarina has also thought ahead about what to do in the unlikely event of a red card. During my coaching career I never really practised for this scenario since I always hoped that none of my players would get sent off. I impressed on my players not to get a red card. Training for that scenario seemed contradictory, but if it ever happened, I knew what I'd do. In the formation I played during the 2022 men's World Cup – depending on the shape of the strikers and the attacking midfielder, but also the tactics of the opponent – I'd continue playing with two strikers and/or have the striker replaced by an attacking midfielder.

Looking back, I was glad that I did have a plan in place. In the seventh minute of the game, Anouk Dekker, our last defender, lost the ball and tried to make up for it by holding back her opponent. Unfortunately, the referee saw it as a foul and gave her a straight red card. I quickly got up from the bench and instructed Merel van Dongen to start warming up. Since I wasn't wearing my glasses, I handed my notebook to Niels de Vries, the exercise physiologist for the Leeuwinnen, and told him where to find the solution. I then shared my thoughts with Arjan and he agreed that Merel would need to come on.

Before each game, our staff and I discuss our possible starting line-ups, as well as those of the opposition, and talk about the various scenarios that could take place during the game. We plan for different situations, such as what we'd do if we took an early lead, if the opposition starts to improvise their game in the last 15 minutes or if they adopt a different formation. We also discuss who will be on the bench and what they can contribute in specific scenarios. If we change our own formation, we decide which tasks need to be adjusted and which players have experience playing in the new formation.

When we're carefully considering all the possible scenarios that could arise, we narrow down each scenario so we're fully aware of the options we have at our disposal if and when they occur. It is then for me and the staff to decide which of the options and scenarios can be used and practised in training games. While we can't always play out every single scenario that might occur during a key fixture or tournament, we focus on dealing with the most important ones. Plan B is only promising if you have trained or played it beforehand, preferably under pressure.

The substitution I made against Spain in that Euro 2022 quarter-final when we were behind 0–1 wasn't a spur-of-the-moment decision. We'd already practised that substitution, and in this particular case it was our Plan B. We'd been eager to try Plan B against strong opposition, and we got the chance to do so during the 2022 Arnold Clark Cup against Germany. We were drawing at the time and needed to win the game to lift the tournament trophy. Before the game we asked some of our players if we should put Plan B into action if the situation demanded it. That would entail taking more risks, even if the scores were level. Fortunately, the players were willing to take the risk, and they became co-owners of the plan. We executed Plan B and went on to beat the Germans 3–1, securing the tournament victory.

Vivianne Miedema, Leeuwinnen forward

Throughout all the years I worked with Sarina there was only one game that stood out where we failed to respond to the opposition. After winning Euro 2017, we played our first friendly against Spain. We went into the game with a lot of self-confidence, but Spain dominated the first half and we struggled to even touch the ball. In our half-time team talk we couldn't figure out what was going wrong – put simply, Spain were better than us in every way.

We didn't have a Plan B to put in place. The difference in quality between the two teams was clear, and we couldn't just rely on confidence to get us a win. Our own expectations and those of the outside world were also higher after our success at the Euros. It was a difficult but necessary reality check for us, and it helped us prepare for the next finals differently.

We don't always go over every possible scenario with the players beforehand because there are simply too many to cover. Instead, the coaching staff prepare for various scenarios so that we can make informed decisions during the game. The players are already familiar with the three most important scenarios – forcing a goal, preventing the opposition from scoring and playing when outnumbered – because we've trained for them extensively in preparation for major tournaments like the Euros or the World Cup.

Another key decision is when to make a substitution during a specific game. This is where gut feeling and strategic thinking come into play. The beauty of football is that every game is unique, but our detailed preparations ensure that we're ready for any situation. Ultimately, it's up to intuition and insight to make the right call at the right moment. Before making a substitution, I always consult with my assistant coaches to get their input based on their own insights and intuitions. However, as head coach the final decision is left to me. I take overall responsibility for the team, so that applies to the substitutions too.

Naturally, we conduct these detailed preparations because we don't have the luxury of discussing substitutions at length during a match. We need to be able to make quick decisions if the situation calls for it. This preparation proved invaluable during the World Cup qualifying play-off final against Switzerland in 2018. If a player receives a red card, emotions can easily get the better of them – and the same goes for me as the coach. However, in that intense moment I had to remain composed and communicate effectively to avoid making mistakes. What helped was Arjan's intervention at halftime. Before we went into the dressing room he took me aside and told me that I seemed overexcited and agitated. He knew that I needed to keep a cool head to prevent my agitation from spreading to the team. Because of his warning, that succeeded. Thanks to our preparations, I was able to stay calm and act decisively, only getting nervous once the substitution had been made.

The final consideration is to evaluate the effectiveness of the substitutions with the coaching staff after the game. We assess whether the substitute was able to successfully implement the intended change, and how it impacted on the team's performance. We also analyse the benefits and possible drawbacks of the substitution, and think about what alternative options may have been more effective given the progression of the game.

Despite this, I have to disappoint Sue Campbell at times when our substitutions don't quite meet expectations. Not every substitution is perfect, however, and sometimes we fall short of expectations. During Euro 2022 with the Lionesses we had a lot of quality players on the bench, so the subs we used had the potential to make a significant impact on the game. Ultimately, the success of any substitution relies on the quality of the team. I strongly believe that my approach to substitution yields better returns among the substitutes, which is why I continue to implement it.

Louis van Gaal, former head coach of the Netherlands men's team

I've never attended one of Sarina's training sessions, but even from a distance I've great admiration for her. She has a dedicated coaching staff, with Arjan Veurink providing tactical support as assistant coach. What impresses me most is that she always comes prepared with multiple game plans in matches – Plan A, Plan B and even Plan C if needed. As a coach myself I understand the importance of having such flexibility. Not every coach possesses this quality, but Sarina does.

During matches, Sarina has the ability to make changes to the starting line-up and smoothly transition to a different playing style by incorporating players with specific skills and attributes. This kind of adaptability is essential in high-level football. It's disappointing to see many coaches simply making like-for-like substitutions without considering the bigger picture. However, Sarina stands out from the rest. In the quarter-finals of Euro 2022, every move she made had been thoroughly planned and rehearsed beforehand.

When I observe the teams she manages, I can truly see her influence as a coach. This is something I believe is crucial for success on the pitch.

TAILORED ANALYSIS

When we prepare for tournaments we dive deep into analysing our potential opponents, with the aim of countering their strengths and exploiting their weaknesses to the fullest extent during the game. We break down each opponent's performance in different phases of play: defence, moments of winning possession, attack and moments of losing possession, as well as in dead-ball situations.

We identify what the opposition does when they have possession, and we analyse the build-up and attacking play. We also analyse how they create their goals, in what formation they play, their approach to building up play, how they position themselves for scoring opportunities and any other significant patterns in their gameplay. We take note of their positional play, whether they typically go wide or prefer a more direct approach.

We also evaluate our opponents' behaviour when they lose possession. Do they apply immediate pressure or fall back? How do they execute their counter-pressing if any patterns exist? Ultimately, we aim to uncover their strengths and weaknesses and determine where we can exploit them. Furthermore, do they have a fluid defending structure or do they remain rigid? Do they press high, sit deep or hold a central position? Are they aggressive from the get-go or do they take a more cautious approach, and how many players forward press? These considerations all need to be factored into our strategy.

We also analyse the moments at which they win possession: do they go on the attack straightaway or attempt to take advantage of positional play? What spaces do they look for when we lose possession and what spaces are created when they transition? Where on the field of play does this occur?

Our process of analysis is incredibly thorough. We discuss and review these analyses with the technical staff to ensure that we're ideally prepared and can effectively work out our challenges and opportunities, and we discuss these at a later stage with the team. Once we've discussed the analysis, I frequently have follow-up questions, often focused on how we can harness our best qualities and expose their weaknesses. By now we are so in tune with each other that the answers to my questions have already been processed or can be given directly. For example, I might ask questions such as how tightly do our opponents defend? Do they assign a specific player for defensive cover and, if so, who is she? Can we find openings in between their defensive lines or should we exploit the space behind their defence? Is there more space in the central area or should we focus on keeping the ball wide, and how do we handle defensive situations in the final third?

In our analyses we also consider the timing of certain situations in the game. For instance, we discovered that in 2019 the United States consistently aimed to score within the first 15 minutes of the game, so they applied intense pressing during that opening period. However, after the first quarter of an hour they reduced their pressing tactics significantly.

Naturally, we also closely examine the characteristics of the key players on the opposing team. We analyse their footballing skills as well as their behaviour on and off the pitch. If anything notable is captured in the footage, we take it into account during our analysis. For example, some players are more adept at dealing with close marking than others, and knowing that this is the case is invaluable.

After completing these detailed analyses we summarise and condense the key points for the players. Our goal is to present the information about our upcoming opponents in a concise manner, taking no more than 20 to 25 minutes maximum. We do this because most players are quite happy to have a short and clear explanation, without going into detail. From experience we've learned that a presentation lasting longer than 25 minutes can be too mentally taxing.

In addition to our observations, we also rely on numeric data to inform our analyses. We use those measurements, for example, to understand and preferably improve the style of play. For example, if we lose the ball, at the moment of transition we want to win the ball back as soon as possible. We keep account of how often that happens and categorize it according to the strength of the opposition. We then plot the corresponding percentages over time to see whether we are actually improving, and to what extent.

Another important aspect of our analysis is identifying opportunities for scoring. We take a detailed look at different types of attacks and examine whether our on-field observations match up with the data we collect. It's about the observations at a team level, but we also narrow in on differences between players who are playing. This information is primarily used by our coaching staff, but we might also share it with the players if we think it can help them see their level of improvement and continue their development accordingly.

During training we also focus on monitoring the players' workload and capacity. Before each session we determine the level of intensity that we want to achieve. During the sessions we keep track of the distance covered by the individual players and the speed at which they run. Afterwards we ask each player to rate their own performance on a scale from 1 to 10.

We use this information to look for patterns or unusual signals. If a player's ratings or data suggest a potential issue, we can talk to the player and/or modify their training to address it. It might be the case that we ask more of a player; alternatively we might also reduce their workload. For example, if we're working on a drill that requires a lot of sprints, the intensity will be different from drills that emphasise endurance. We take this into account when creating our training plans, as exercises that require short bursts of energy will require longer recovery times than ones that focus on endurance. By creating a good programme and by doing the right things both on and off the pitch, we aim to keep players in top form and feeling fresh, and to minimise the chances of injuries.

The use of data is crucial for our coaching staff to support and validate our observations on the pitch. When necessary we can make adjustments during training drills to vary the intensity level.

INNOVATION UNDER TIME PRESSURE

In our line of work, time is always against us. We constantly have to decide what to prioritise and what to exclude, including new ideas, trends and advances in (women's) football.

We can't experiment with every single innovation that's introduced, but we aim to identify the ones that are most important for our own development. These cover various areas that contribute to team performance, such as nutrition, equipment, psychology and tactical innovation.

I'd love to spend more time on these. I hardly get round to watching games between the biggest clubs which don't have my players in them. I find the latest trends interesting and then ask myself whether these are innovations we might be able to adopt with our own team. Many teams, for example, play with a full back who moves into the middle, thus forming a rectangle in midfield.

The business world pays great attention to innovations, sometimes coming up with radical ideas. While these interest me, they often lie beyond my scope as my job is to contribute to the development of women's football. People do see me as an innovator, and even though I find this depiction a little extreme, I certainly feel that innovations and advances are necessary to improve performance. These might involve using new training techniques to enhance fitness and stamina or adopting nutritional supplements used in other sports to sustain high-intensity play for longer periods.

Within the coaching staff we divide responsibilities to keep track of the most significant innovations in our respective areas of expertise. If we find an innovation that's particularly interesting and relevant for an upcoming tournament, we discuss it in staff meetings well in advance. We evaluate its potential impact on performance and how we might implement it, and based on our assessment we decide whether to pursue it or not.

We embrace challenges for both players and staff, as innovations bring energy to the team and foster overall growth. For instance, we worked on revamping our throw-ins and brought in a specialist to demonstrate novel techniques. We incorporated these changes into our preparations for the 2023 World Cup, giving us a better chance of retaining possession and creating scoring opportunities.

The 2023 World Cup posed a unique challenge due to the long flight from the UK to Australia and New Zealand and the more than ten-hour time difference. We called in expert help and referred to it as the 'Beat the Jet Lag' project. To combat the effects of jet lag, we provided players and staff with strategies and resources. We adapted our training-camp schedule in England to reflect whether each player was more of an early bird or a night owl, adjusting their diet and eating times accordingly. Players also used special glasses that modified their sleep patterns. Every little improvement we made increased our chance of success.

We also relied on external research, such as studies conducted by the Sports Medicine and Sports Science Department at the FA that focuses on knee injuries in women and girls. As many players are unable to participate in club matches or even the World Cup due to such injuries, this is a crucial and urgent concern.

I believe it is crucial to thoroughly investigate multiple areas. We need to explore what a player's typical day looks like, their footballing schedule, the training they undergo and the different types of support available to them, such as medical care, mental and emotional guidance, their physical well-being and educational opportunities. What is the player's lifestyle?

SUPER-STRENGTHS OF THE TEAM DEMAND LEADERSHIP

Prior to a tournament, as coaching staff we rarely work with fixed groups within the squad. While we do work extensively with groups, we purposefully put them together based on what we want to achieve in any particular session. We conduct tactical meetings, team development sessions and meetings that focus on specific aspects of the game with the players, as well as holding one-on-one discussions.

On the pitch, although there's always one player who wears the captain's armband, I also work with a group of leading players, typically four or five individuals who are more experienced and vocal. They serve as leaders both on and off the pitch and must possess the ability to read the game well while also attending to team tasks in general. It's important to note that these players don't hold a more prominent status within the team, as leadership can manifest in a variety of ways.

In the run-up to a tournament, our coaching staff never work with fixed groups within the team selection. I work closely with them to test out various aspects of our strategy, such as key scenarios that often arise in matches. This process is tailored to each individual player, as going through every scenario with the entire team can lead to information overload. During preparations, we analyse ways in which each player can maximise their performance and contribute to the team's success.

Leah Williamson, Lionesses defender (captain in Euro 2022)

From the moment I first spoke with Sarina I felt a deep sense of respect and comfort in being able to share everything with her. This hasn't always been the case with other coaches I've had – typically, I wait and observe before opening up to a new coach. But with Sarina things were different.

During our first training camp Sarina had one-on-one sessions with all of the players. In her direct, honest way – which can be unusual in British culture – she asked me about my career goals and personal traits, and my family background from when I was growing up. For some reason I felt comfortable opening up to her and revealing all of my thoughts and emotions. We established a transparent and sincere relationship from the start.

Later on she asked me if I wanted to be the team's captain. I was surprised because I'd never held that position before. I believed that leadership was partly dependent on others' perceptions of you. So when Sarina suggested it would be a good step for me, I agreed to take on the challenge. I said I would [have to] disappoint her if she thought I needed to change, because I wanted to be who I am. Her response put me at ease. Honestly, I didn't feel capable of changing into a leader. 'I just want you to be yourself,' she reassured me. This was the best gift she could give me – she expressed belief and confidence in my abilities.

Of course, I knew I'd grow and develop as a player and as a professional while being part of the team. But what really stood out to me was when Sarina asked me to provide feedback whenever necessary – both individually and as part of a team. This made me feel comfortable about sharing my thoughts and opinions without any reservations. Even when Sarina shares a problem with us, she always listens carefully to what the staff and players say before making a final decision. I feel like my role in the team and within the staff is highly appreciated and valued.

The team development sessions are an essential part of our preparation for tournaments. Each session revolves around a specific theme, such as 'team values' or 'winning behaviours', which we discuss in detail with the group. The sessions are meticulously planned in collaboration with Kate Hays, our head of performance psychology. She's an authority in the field of sports psychology, who helps us carefully structure and design their content.

Together with Kate, we plan the structure and content of our team development programmes, as well as determine the optimal sub-group distribution for sessions. Our aim is to achieve a well-balanced player distribution across sub-groups. In most cases, but sometimes deliberately not, one of the players from the leaders' group will participate in a sub-group. Furthermore, we aim to foster an inclusive environment where players who might not ordinarily provide input are encouraged to share their ideas.

Lucy Bronze, Lionesses defender

Sarina and I share some similarities. We both know exactly what we want and we're highly motivated to achieve it. When we first started working together, however, we had to figure out how our personalities would complement each other. Since both of us are result-oriented and direct communicators, it mostly works out, although it could sometimes be challenging.

Being driven and result-oriented has its difficulties, but Sarina inspires me to persevere. Her drive is contagious and motivates everyone around her. With Sarina, I feel comfortable expressing my drive without holding back. To me, direct communication is a crucial aspect of leadership. Although Sarina is straightforward, it's supported by a strong connection she has with her players and staff. This bond fosters an environment in which she can convey feedback that emphasises player development.

Sarina has a talent for delivering straightforward and easy-to-understand messages. Her clarity is crucial for me. Sometimes her feedback may not be what you want to hear, but you always know what it means and what steps you need to take to improve for the next time. In a leadership position, this kind of transparency is vital for building a successful team, whether in sports or in business.

There have been plenty of times when I haven't been happy with what Sarina had to say. I could choose to dwell on it, but I find it more beneficial to use her feedback in a positive way.

While we typically distribute the leadership group across various groups, there are times when we intentionally keep them together. For example, during the follow-up evaluation of the Arnold Clark Cup tournament, the leadership group was given the chance to present their assessment of what went well and what didn't. This exercise was aimed at promoting awareness among the team and reducing the players' dependence on coaching staff. We believe that players making the necessary adjustments themselves on the pitch can often be more effective than waiting for us to dictate from the touchline.

Millie Bright, Lionesses defender (captain)

The team's communication really improved over time. When we're playing in a stadium packed with fans, it's crucial that we can communicate effectively with each other if the match calls for it. In the lead-up to Euro 2022, we took multiple steps in that direction. We achieved this by establishing a secure space where every player can freely express themselves without fear of judgement or feeling like their voice doesn't matter. In our team, everyone is treated equally and their opinions are valued.

For every game we spend a lot of time doing analysis as a team. We all have a chance to contribute whenever it's necessary, but ultimately Sarina is the one in charge. She makes the final decisions on what we'll do. And she's really good at that. There are no grey areas for her – she's completely clear about the game plan and what she expects from us as a team. Because everyone can express their opinions, the players feel more valued, and we all have a sense of ownership over the plan. I think it is vital to have a coach who provides confidence and freedom to be yourself as a player and as a person. Sarina has created an unbelievable culture and environment at England, and I really believe it has allowed us to gel even more and contributed to getting the best out of us as players and as a team.

In preparation for the 2023 World Cup, we organised a session with Kate focused on the team's 'super-strengths' and their potential pitfalls, and we asked different groups to identify what they thought these were. This exercise provided valuable feedback, especially as it enabled players who would otherwise have kept quiet in the larger group sessions to share their opinions. Through this process we as the coaching staff gained significant information about not only our strengths and weaknesses, but also about the group dynamics within the team.

Time is scarce with national teams, so we want to use the time we have to spend on team development as best and effectively as possible. We try to improve that every time. For example, in preparation for the 2023 World Cup, we noticed that the same groups were formed too often during training. When new players joined the part of the team we had been working with for a long time, we saw that the new players sought each other out. This left them in the first phase of team development. As staff, we took more control and organised the groups differently, which created a better balance between the players who had been in the selection for a longer time and the new players.

Lucy Bronze, Lionesses defender

How often do people challenge their boss? In my opinion it should happen more frequently. When you have a relationship with your manager that allows for respectful challenges, it often improves the overall connection between you. And when that happens, it also benefits the team. This is what makes Sarina such a great coach. Despite being the boss, she is always open to listening and taking action based on what others say. She remains true to herself and is straightforward with those around her.

Three months after she joined the Lionesses we had another conversation after I got injured. One of her observations was that not many people were speaking up during team meetings. I mentioned that some players were afraid of her, to which Sarina responded that she wasn't really that intimidating. We had a laugh about it because, despite her height, Sarina didn't seem scary to me at all. However, being the boss carries weight in England, and this realisation prompted her to seek out more people who would challenge her. I'm happy to fulfil that role.

I believe that in England we need more time to establish the kind of communication that is commonplace in the Netherlands, where players like Vivianne Miedema were able to confidently express their opinions. In recent years I've been part of the group of players who've taken on a leadership role, and I feel comfortable in that position. Since Sarina became our coach we've actively tried to challenge her more, which is something she explicitly encouraged. Some players have had to learn how to do this, but it comes naturally to me. I've been part of leading clubs that compete for championships, and I value the ability to have open discussions with the coach, even if they're challenging.

THE SQUAD IS THE TEAM

We prioritise giving equal attention to every member of the squad, as we're aware that winning any tournament is a collective effort involving every player's contribution. In every game I put out the best team, which doesn't always mean fielding the best players. I might sometimes leave certain players on the bench at the start of the game because I know they'll have an impact if I bring them on later.

Given that the squad can comprise up to 23 players, this can be a challenging task. We're fortunate to have a range of talented players to choose from, and our selection process is based on the opponent we're playing. I always ensure a safe environment, but I am in charge of a top-level sports team. My choices are always geared towards winning as a team rather than promoting individual players.

Arjan Veurink, Lionesses assistant coach

I'd previously worked closely with at least eight players in the Leeuwinnen squad and had a strong bond with some of them, so it was natural for them to come to see me first if something was bothering them. Initially, Sarina found this complicated. She questioned why they'd come to me instead

225

of her, and she had concerns about what was happening behind her back.

I understood her perspective, but since we'd worked together for a long time it was only natural for these players to turn to me. At that point, however, Sarina and I didn't know each other well enough to be confident about this dynamic. It's all part of the uncertainty that comes with a recent promotion.

I made it clear to Sarina, the coaching staff and the team that my role was as an assistant. I tried to fulfil that role to the best of my abilities. But I also believed in teamwork. If I couldn't contribute in that way anymore, I might as well step down. I conveyed the same message to the players. They could share anything with me, knowing that it would be in complete confidence, although at the end of the conversation I'd always ask the player what I could share with Sarina and what needed to remain private. We'd also discuss any steps the player could take to address the issue themselves or make it a subject of discussion.

Generally, these conversations focused on three main topics. The first was about the players themselves, including their happiness, the attention they were receiving and any current developments concerning them. The second topic was the team as a whole – how the players interacted, the team's performance and any decisions that still needed to be made. The final topic revolved around tactical matters –

players feeling restricted in their positions, needing more support on the pitch or desiring more freedom in their roles.

Engaging in these discussions was challenging because it meant finding the right balance between maintaining confidentiality and recognising when action was necessary as part of the coaching staff. This is why I emphasised transparency not only with the players but also with Sarina and the rest of the staff. I made it clear what I could and couldn't share. It also placed significant strain on the trust between Sarina and me. However, we managed to navigate this effectively because Sarina was prepared to reflect on things, and together we learned how to handle these situations.

We also established a work rhythm that facilitated these conversations. We'd start each morning by discussing the day's programme, which provided an opportune moment for anyone in the squad to express any concerns they might have.

In each game, the squad is always split into two groups. 11 players start the match, while 12 remain on the bench, so the coaching staff need to focus on managing this situation effectively. Every player has their own 'individual development plan', which includes footage from matches and training sessions. We make sure we have conversations with each player, although who conducts these can vary. Most players place more importance on speaking with the head coach, so we take that into consideration. While that was the case in the Netherlands, it's even more so in England. We plan and set goals for these conversations to guide our approach. Most of the discussions about individual development plans are led by the assistant coach and goalkeeping coach, with only a few done by myself. We want to help the whole squad in their development. We also believe that the whole squad is essential for winning a tournament. Every player deserves to be seen and appreciated, so that's what we prioritise.

If the reserve players are training on the day after a match, I make sure that I'm out there with them too. I know that not every coach does this, but I feel it's important to be around during training sessions, to watch the training process and to stay in touch. What's the intensity of the training and what level of performance do the players attain? Most of the time I simply observe, which gives the players a sense of being noticed as well. This group of reserve players needs to be ready to step up when there are injuries or tactical changes during a game, which is why I want to be present at every training session.

In every tournament, every player knows what their position in the team is when they are brought on during a match. They also know which players are ahead of them and what they need to do to improve their chances of being selected in the starting line-up. This transparency is highly valued by the players, even if they may not always agree with their relative position in the pecking order. In the conversations I have with players my aim is to build trust while focusing on both the positive aspects of their play and areas for improvement.

Jill Scott, Lionesses midfielder

The moment you found out whether you'd made the squad was nerve-wracking. Sarina chose to deliver the news in a live conversation, which was different from my previous ten international tournaments. I'd usually receive an email or a phone call from the coach, informing me about the selection – it was never done in real time.

Waiting for Sarina to call me in made me incredibly anxious and I'd already drunk four cups of coffee during that time. Finally, the door opened and it was my turn. This was the moment when I'd find out if I'd be part of the team heading to Euro 2022.

As expected, the meeting with Sarina was direct but always respectful. It wasn't an easy task for her either. She had to deliver either good or bad news. If it was bad news, the meeting was usually short and there was a car ready to take the player home. If it was good news, we'd gather with the rest of the squad to celebrate and share our relief and joy.

The way Sarina carried herself during these meetings reflected her conviction. Even though it was challenging for her, she believed in her plan and knew who was crucial for its success. The clarity she brought to these conversations made it clear where each player stood within the team.

At that point Sarina made it clear that I'd made the squad, but I wouldn't be in the starting line-up. My role would be to conserve my energy as a substitute player and support the team off the pitch. This was never a problem for me, as I've always taken that role seriously. In a tournament setting, it's vital to fight for everyone and check in with all of the players on the team, especially when you're travelling together for weeks on end. I enjoy doing that and always have the well-being of the group in mind.

During our meeting, Sarina added that my role was not just off-the-pitch support. She stressed the importance of my on-pitch contribution, which was a huge boost to my confidence as a player. Whenever I stepped onto the pitch, I held myself to a high standard and gave my all for the team. My positive attitude has always been an essential part of my game, so when I came off the bench I made sure to bring extra energy to the pitch. If I sensed that the energy levels of the team were dwindling, I stepped up to the challenge and made an extra sprint or delivered a heavy tackle to boost the team's energy.

Sarina's instructions were clear: I needed to increase the energy levels of the team, both on and off the pitch. During that meeting I made the decision to give my all for the team, no matter what my role was.

When I have to decide not to put a player in the starting line-up or not pick them at all, a detailed conversation doesn't work – because of heightened emotions the player may not hear what I have to say so I keep it concise. The specifics can wait for a later stage. It's natural for everyone to want to start, especially in a major tournament. These conversations are difficult for me because I know I'll be disappointing someone. But it's part of my job, and I've become better at handling these situations. All players have their own emotions and opinions, and it's vital for them to be given the time in which to process these feelings and thoughts, and come to accept their role within the overall set-up.

Vivianne Miedema, Leeuwinnen forward

Sarina is a determined and strong-willed individual. When I think of her, the words 'headstrong' and 'tenacious' come to mind. She has an unwavering focus on accomplishing her goals, and she won't let anything get in her way. This single-mindedness has both its advantages and disadvantages. As a team we benefited from her drive – no matter the situation, we always had a plan in place. This gave us confidence on the pitch and enabled us to remain calm even in challenging moments. We knew that Sarina and the coaching staff had prepared us well, and we believed we could turn things around when faced with adversity.

Having said that, I can imagine it hasn't always been easy for Sarina's family, as she has dedicated so much time and effort to football over the years. I also felt that her focus was primarily on a core group of 13 or 14 players on the pitch. We often discussed how to keep those players who rarely got a chance to play motivated. Between 2017 and 2021 Sarina recognised this challenge and made adjustments. For example, she ensured that the first training session after a game was significant for players who'd sat it out on the bench, giving them attention and making them feel important. I'm sure that she made further changes when she transitioned to coaching the Lionesses. Sarina is a coach who welcomes feedback and embraces learning opportunities.

For me, she should relax more often and enjoy what she's accomplished with her teams. While her tunnel vision brought us great success, it's important to step outside of that intense focus every now and then. Working with Sarina can be quite intense, which is why moments of relaxation are even more valuable.

The most important thing is that I can reflect on matters and know that I've got complete respect for the players. There are moments that are tough for me as well, where I have to deal with the emotional toll that comes with being a coach. I care for the players and all their actions, their every movement, their comings and goings.

To be honest, I sometimes question whether I'm cut out for this job. It's difficult to disappoint players who put in a supreme effort day in, day out, hoping to play or make it to a tournament as part of the squad. I strive to support their development as players and their desire to contribute to the team's success but there always comes a time when I have to tell a player that, at that particular moment, they've been overlooked in favour of a teammate. Elite sports can be cruel, and dropping players out of the matchday team or sidelining them altogether deeply hurts me every time. It takes a toll on me emotionally and drains my energy as I genuinely care for the players and understand what they go through.

I care deeply about the team, my staff and the people around me. I try to be as clear as possible about expectations, opportunities and progress in my team's development so that together we can achieve our dreams.

Every day I learn to do things better, and that's what I want. I know I can come across as matter-of-fact sometimes, but I'm a woman who feels deeply.

I firmly believe in building a strong connection with my players. It's crucial to have a bond that can withstand the ups and downs, where we still maintain respect and appreciation for each other even if someone doesn't play or get selected. That's something I value enormously. I constantly reflect on whether there was more I could have done, if I've been honest, if I've given my best for the team, and if I'm willing to be vulnerable in order to learn and grow. As long as I can answer 'yes' to those questions, then I feel like I'm suited to this role. But I have to admit, selecting a team is painful every single time.

10

THE POWER OF
LETTING GO

As members of the coaching staff we all strongly believe that we can contribute to the development of our players. The time we have with our players is limited, however, as for the most part they spend their time with their own clubs. We can still make them aware of certain issues and encourage them to think about their development. Our approach is based on their 'individual development plan', mentioned earlier in this book.

As the national team, we operate in an interesting context. Over the course of a football season many things happen within our field of vision, but many more happen outside our field of vision. When players are with their clubs, we often have limited sight of their progress. Conversely, when they are with us, we can take a close look at their performance, but there are still aspects that we may miss. It's during these periods that we aim to exercise a lot of influence, including on the processes invisible to us.

THE IMPORTANCE OF PITCH OBSERVATION

Our guiding principle is to evaluate what we observe on the pitch. We work closely with the team to define the expectations and tasks for each player during games. This includes not only how they are fulfilling their roles, but also the way in which they handle setbacks and disappointments during matches. We define the boundaries of these expectations and engage in discussions with the players.

Players earn credit on the pitch for good performances, not everything gets discussed at the time it occurs. For instance, if a player like Vivianne Miedema scores a goal every game, we won't criticise her when an opponent manages to get past her once in a while during a transition. Similarly, if Lieke Martens makes several crucial crosses, we won't have a go at her if she finds it tough to defend against an opponent's pressure on a single occasion. If Beth Mead makes decisive moves, she doesn't get censured if now and again she pushes up too far. And if Lucy Bronze is so dangerous in attack that she creates good chances, it may happen that she's not able to fall back into defence in good time. I trust in the players' knowledge and skills, and understand that this is all part of the game.

Sometimes, players may fail to follow the agreed-upon strategies for an extended period or they behave inappropriately in a way that harms the team. Then a conversation will follow. Incidentally, I notice soon enough when this is needed. In such cases, we have no choice but to intervene. We keep a close eye on the team and pay attention to all the tell-tale signs that suggest something needs addressing.

In the end, it's not about the players being able to handle us, as the coaching staff, but the other way around. We try to find ways to handle each player according to their individual styles. It sometimes requires patience on our part when you see something happening, especially off the pitch. But it is mainly about what we observe on the pitch.

We're highly attuned to each other within the Lionesses staff, enabling us to observe and influence the players' behaviours in a structured manner. We have daily meetings where we discuss everything flagged by the players' performances and strategise actions aimed at their development. During these meetings, we also determine which staff member will specifically focus on which player. Thus, we agree that initially, for example, Arjan Veurink or Geraint Twose will have those conversations. If necessary

I can take over the conversation at a later stage to check on whether the message has had any impact, to compliment the player if there has been an improvement or to comment if we notice insufficient progress.

So we try to help the players by mirroring them, influencing their behaviour, making agreements, setting and monitoring boundaries. We are not perfect ourselves either.

Lieke Martens, Leeuwinnen forward

As players, we mainly focus on our own clubs during the regular football season. But something remarkable happens when we come together during the Leeuwinnen's training camps – the intensity and skill level get pushed to new heights. Sarina sensed this and set the bar even higher for us. She expected more from us when she was coach. In the past, she might have been OK with a ball going out of bounds, but this changed when she took the helm of the national team. Sarina knew our abilities inside out. She saw the growth of the team, so demanded more of the team.

Sarina has a bold and straightforward approach when communicating with players. It's one of her defining strengths as a top-level coach. Initially, I found it a bit challenging to adapt to, as she comes from the Randstad in the centre of the Netherlands while I come from a small village in the south. Our worlds seemed vastly different, especially considering her direct communication style, although I soon grew to value her candour.

Above all, I'm incredibly proud of Sarina. Her impact on women's football, both in the Netherlands and beyond, is immense. Personally, I've always enjoyed working with her. Whenever foreign players ask me about her coaching, I can't help but speak highly of her. Sarina's passion for women's football is unparalleled, and she has wholeheartedly dedicated herself to her teams. It's truly inspiring to witness, from my time up close with the Leeuwinnen to now observing from a slight distance with the Lionesses.

I've played a lot under her leadership. Her trust enabled me to grow and flourish, and I'm incredibly grateful to her for that. However, I never had many meetings with Sarina. Building a connection with your coach doesn't always happen through talking; I just feel that we had that connection. It was a mutual relationship that brought about so much beauty.

Sarina is not only a good coach, but she's also a good person. She doesn't need to be liked by everyone, but she does value respecting everyone. That's important to her. She can tell a player in one sentence that she doesn't need her today but that she's still important to the team. A short-term decision doesn't mean she's no longer there for you. Not every coach has that.

PERSONAL PREPAREDNESS FOR PEAK PERFORMANCE

The responsibility for getting ready for a game rests on each individual player's shoulders. They must take the initiative themselves to be optimally prepared and decide what they're going to do to ensure that they are. Different players have their own unique methods of preparation, and we encourage them in this by collaborating with our staff to determine what resources players can use in their preparations. In fact, we employ a technique called 'nudging'; we encourage the players to prepare in a professional manner, but they have the freedom to make their own choices.

When we have tournament games there may be a four-day gap between the previous match and the upcoming one. We refer to these days as match day +1, match day +2, match day −2 and match day −1. The designations +1, +2, −2 and −1 indicate the number of days after or before a game. What exactly do players do in the four days between two matches to recover and get ready for the next one?

They know pretty well what they must do to be fresh again for the next game. Right after the final whistle, they will ensure they eat and drink adequately to aid in their initial recovery, even before we return to the hotel. Once back at the hotel, they consume a specially prepared sports meal to further support their recovery. The remainder of the evening and the following day (match day +1) are dedicated to treatments provided by the medical staff, ice baths, cycling to cool down and exercises in the gym.

The next day (match day +2) is essentially a free day to ensure they feel mentally refreshed. This is especially important when players are spending extended periods together during tournaments. They appreciate having their own space and being able to think about other things apart from football. It's also the day when family and friends can visit, which most players find rejuvenating. They go through so much in just a few weeks that it's nice to be able to share these experiences with their loved ones.

The following day marks two days before the next game (match day −2). This is when we discuss tactics for the upcoming match. In the morning we have a meeting in which we analyse the strengths and weaknesses of the opposing team, and determine what these mean for our own team. We share our game plan and focus on key players from the other team. Arjan always leads this discussion in a way that encourages interaction with the players. He asks for possible solutions to the tactical challenges we'll face in the forthcoming game. We already have a plan in mind, but it's important to get the players to take responsibility for their own performances.

Once we have discussed the opposition, we almost always have an 11 against 11 training. As far as possible, one of the teams imitates the tactics of our upcoming opponents. Additionally, we create video footage of the opposing team, which players can request from the coaching staff in order to prepare. It's important to remember that less is more. We avoid overwhelming the players with excessive information, preferring to keep conversations concise and avoiding getting too caught up in details. We sometimes engage in discussions about specific positions, but this is the exception rather than the rule. We can discuss anything if requested, but that will obviously depend on the players. Our influence as staff members is minimal in these situations.

We have a playlist of video clips for each of the opposing team's players, showcasing both their strengths and weaknesses, and our players get the opportunity to watch them at a convenient time during the day. After the tactical talk, if needed, we almost always meet individually with each player. Match day −2 also allows for extra downtime, rest and proper nutrition. As a tournament progresses, these all become increasingly important.

I am also keen on keeping everyone in good physical condition. During the 2019 World Cup we had to play the final against the United States just four days after winning the semi-final against Sweden in extra-time. Recovering from matches during a tournament is one of the most important activities for the team.

The training session on the day before the game (match day −1) is usually the same. We call it the 'confidence' session, a pleasant training session for the players. It's a quick and targeted session without much additional information on the opposing team. Players should finish the session on a high note and feel confident heading into the game.

On the night before the game I'll reveal the starting line-up. If necessary, I'll show more clips from the tactical training we did the previous day to emphasise the importance of performing well. Only the most critical talking points are presented and reiterated. On game day itself, we discuss set pieces. The players must learn for themselves what they need to prepare for each fixture or opponent. Anything you can imagine, we facilitate. But it starts with the player asking the question: what nutrition do I need, what treatment do I need, how do I prepare myself for the opponent's tactics? We try to encourage that, but we don't prescribe it and assume the responsibilities.

PURSUIT OF A DREAM

I'm committed to giving everything I have to achieve our dream of winning, and I expect the same level of dedication from both the players and staff I work with. That's why I choose to work with top athletes – it's the way I like to collaborate. This mindset has been with me since my days playing football.

Leah Williamson, Lionesses defender (captain in Euro 2022)

Making our dream the focal point of Euro 2022 felt absolutely right. It was uncharted territory for us, especially since the tournament was taking place on our home turf. The expectations were high – everyone believed we would come out as winners. But why should we have any special right to win over other countries? We were well aware that we had the talent and skill to win, but before reaching the final we had to clear every hurdle along the way. That meant taking it step by step, match by match. Winning the semi-final was our next goal, but we couldn't overlook any opponents on the journey. We understood that each victory brought us closer to our ultimate goal – lifting the trophy in the final. It was an arduous path, but we were determined to give it our all and make our dream come true.

Achieving one's dream requires developing a strong belief in oneself. In that moment we had the perfect formula to do just that. After every training session Sarina reminded us of our hard work and determination, and that we never complained. No training session ever went to waste. Her confidence in us grew with each session, and that gave us the confidence we needed to win. I remember feeling the same way during the quarter-final match against Spain. It was then that I knew we were going to win. I felt a clear sense that we could go all the way and take home the victory. Throughout the game, I never felt any pressure or stress. There was no way we could lose. We also understood that we were playing for millions of people across the globe. It was different from before, when no one had ever heard of us. This realisation, especially during the match against Spain, proved to be the turning point in the tournament.

After winning Euro 2022 we started to feel like everyone – the fans, the media – believed that we were also going to win the World Cup a year later. But on what basis? Once again, it was uncharted territory for us. Just like the previous year's Euros, we'd never been in a World Cup final before, let alone won it. The tournament was being held in Australia and New Zealand, which presented a completely different setting from a home tournament, and that's not to mention how far we had to travel from the UK to get there, the vast distances between the various host cities and the Antipodean climate – the tournament was taking place in July and August, the southern hemisphere's winter.

The major difference, however, was that suddenly more people were talking about the World Cup and the England team. Despite all these changes, our approach remained relatively unchanged. We had a successful blueprint for dealing with expectations, based on realising our next dream. We'd approach this new tournament step by step, one game at a time.

MEASURES FOR PREVENTING DISAPPOINTMENTS

One of the most significant shifts in mentality that I discussed with the team was around the pressure they placed upon themselves. Some of them would say that they'd always win with the Lionesses, but when this was shown not to be the case, both fans and the media were disappointed. I made the players aware that we could avoid such reactions by refraining from vocalising our desire to win. Instead, we should simply focus on delivering our finest football, giving it our all. Naturally, we'd still aim to win every game we played, but we wouldn't be proclaiming from the rooftops that we were destined to prevail in the Euros or the World Cup.

This wasn't merely a matter of words; it represented a genuine shift in mindset. Our main focus became what we had to do in the forthcoming match, and I noticed that it really removed a great deal of pressure from the shoulders of certain players. This approach also increased our chance of winning and of bringing joy to the fans. We were focused fully on the process, not on the end result, and during Euro 2022 it proved to be immensely successful. Not once did anyone suggest that we'd emerge as champions of the tournament. We simply concentrated on our plan and in doing so we went all the way. This marked a truly substantial change, one that I still cherish, even though it wasn't embraced by everyone in the same manner.

Louis van Gaal, former head coach of the Netherlands men's team

In 2022 I made a deliberate choice to publicly announce that the explicit aim of the Dutch men's team was to become world champions, a departure from my previous tenure as national coach in 2014, when I refrained from such pronouncements. Back then I was working with a less experienced group and there was no benefit in stating our goal of winning the World Cup.

This time the situation was different. I had a highly talented group of players, many of whom had eight to ten years' experience at the top level and trophies to their name, so it made no sense to present our pursuit of the World Cup as merely a dream. Of course, as a coach it was a risk to take this approach. The increasing media attention has made it challenging for coaches to do their jobs effectively, which is why many of them prefer not to communicate openly. However, with players like Virgil van Dijk, Nathan Aké, Frenkie de Jong and Memphis Depay, I felt that I'd be doing both them and myself a disservice by not aiming for the top and being transparent about it.

Sarina, with both the Leeuwinnen and the Lionesses, chose not to publicly declare her goal of winning the tournaments she's taken part in. This approach relieves some pressure from the team, especially when they're still gaining experience. I wonder if she'll continue in the same vein in the future as she works with a more experienced squad.

Every now and then I share a light-hearted joke about my will to win with Anja van Ginhoven, general manager of the Lionesses team. Our paths first crossed on the pitch at a significant moment. I was playing a league game for my team KFC '71 against Ter Leede, where Anja was playing. During the game I was involved in a fierce duel with Anja and unintentionally stepped on her foot. It was an intense clash, but unfortunately she had the worst of it. She not only suffered a bruised metatarsal bone but also dislocated her shoulder as she fell. Her shoulder injury was so severe that it took her several months to fully recover. As a reminder of our first encounter, she developed a wrist condition known as piano key syndrome, a testament to this once dislocated shoulder.

Sadly, my team got relegated that season. Being an international player, it was important for me to continue competing at the highest level in the Netherlands. As fate would have it, I ended up joining Ter Leede, where I had the chance to meet Anja once again.

Anja van Ginhoven, general manager of the Lionesses

How can I even begin to describe Sarina in just a few words? Well, here goes: she's incredibly dedicated and approachable, and she always puts the interests of the team and their development first. This has been true since the very first day I met her 25 years ago, and remains the case to this day. Sarina is never about herself, she's always focused on what's best for the team. Even as a player, she acted as an extension of the coach on the pitch. Her main concern was always how to implement tactics and improve the team's performance to increase their chances of winning.

Back in those days I was mostly focused on my own performance on the pitch. I also had a busy social life that I thoroughly enjoyed. But when Sarina arrived at Ter Leede, everything changed, both for the team and for me. She was the missing piece we needed at that time with her unwavering dedication to the sport, her constant focus on developing the team and her relentless will to win it all. We could talk about it and we could each try it individually – or we could come together, learn from each other and do it as a team. And with Sarina, we chose the latter.

THE POWER OF LETTING GO

My collaboration with Arjan Veurink began in February 2017, and it has been quite a ride. I knew him as the coach of one of my former rivals, FC Twente, but I didn't know him very well. Our collaboration went well in its first six months and that gave me confidence for the future.

Euro 2017 marked my first experience as a national head coach. I had to find my own way initially. I needed time to figure out what leadership at this level was all about and what style worked best for me. As a first-time head coach of a national team, it was important for me to make the position my own before delegating responsibilities to my staff. Honestly, I found and still find it difficult to let go. When I coached ADO Den Haag, I was used to doing everything myself. It was hard work, but I was comfortable because I knew I could deliver quality. The challenge for me in 2017 and 2018 was learning how to loosen my control over every aspect of the team, and this didn't come naturally.

Louis van Gaal, former head coach of the Netherlands men's team

Sarina and I share a common struggle when it comes to letting go. Like Sarina, in the beginning I used to handle everything myself because I'd then have confidence that it would meet the highest standards. I simply trusted myself more than others, but we both had to learn the importance of delegating responsibilities to the coaching staff.

As I started working with a permanent staff consisting of specialists, things gradually improved. The only thing I always maintained full control over was the tactical preparations before a game. I was responsible for coaching the first team, while Danny Blind took charge of the reserves.

His role was to study and analyse the playing style of our upcoming opponents, ensuring that we were thoroughly prepared. Each member of the coaching staff had specific instructions to closely track an assigned player and alert the team with a whistle to pause the game if the player made a particular action. At that point my assistant or I would explain in detail what had just happened and how it could have been done better.

Sarina follows a similar approach in training during tournaments. It serves as a means of building a cohesive and effective team so that every member of the coaching staff, not just the head coach, can communicate what we expect from the players. During post-training evaluations, all staff members are encouraged to voice their opinions and contribute. This is because coaching remains a collaborative effort.

Arjan and I got to know each other well, and fortunately it turned out that our football philosophies largely aligned. This was a prerequisite that we had discussed in our initial conversations, and it proved to hold true in practice. However, I quickly noticed that Arjan couldn't fully express his creativity in his role. During our discussions, he'd sometimes struggle to understand what I wanted, even though I knew he had valuable ideas of his own.

Arjan Veurink, Leeuwinnen assistant coach

In late December 2016 Sarina gave me a call and mentioned that she was looking for an assistant coach. She'd approached me before about a job with the Dutch FA, but at that time I'd already committed to FC Twente and had to decline the offer. Now the circumstances were different. After the 2015/16 season I'd finished with FC Twente and was considering my future options. It was a good opportunity to have a discussion.

I went into the meeting with an open mind. I was curious to hear Sarina's plans, and I'd heard that she also wanted Foppe de Haan as an assistant. As we talked, Sarina showed the same passion and clarity that I'd seen from her on the touchline. We discussed our respective footballing visions, and I was particularly interested in hearing about hers, including how she planned to continue implementing the principles and tactics of the Leeuwinnen.

One of the things that really resonated with me was when Sarina expressed her desire to keep taking the team in the same direction. I agreed with her that it was important to have a solid foundation before making any drastic changes. With the limited time that we had before the Euros, it would have been risky to disrupt the team dynamics. However, I also noticed that there was still room for applying these principles and tactics in different ways. I'd a feeling that I approached the game with a greater freedom than Sarina did, which could lead to some interesting discussions.

Above all, the most crucial factor was that we had a connection. We both felt that our collaboration had the potential to become something special. It was a risk we were taking, as our sense of an affinity for each other was based on just one meeting and initial impressions. Soon enough, I realised that Sarina had a talent for surrounding herself with capable individuals. For example, Foppe de Haan was a highly experienced coach who'd previously been appointed by Sarina as an assistant, and I believe that it takes a strong individual to do that. However, just because we clicked didn't mean that our characters were the same. If anything, we were quite different and would sometimes clash in the beginning due to our different reactions to situations. Nonetheless, we always approached working together with mutual respect and with the shared goal of improving the team's quality. This is why our collaboration proved to be effective.

The new collaboration with Arjan was at times quite challenging for both of us. This was partly due to his transition from head coach to assistant coach. However, those who know Arjan well are aware that when he accepts a role, he puts his heart and soul into it. As a result, he conscientiously performed his duties as an assistant coach, which sometimes meant that he had to restrain himself – and I noticed this. Whereas in his previous position he'd certainly be a vocal type of coach during a game, he now stayed quiet. This was for my benefit, and I could see that he was trying to avoid creating any ambiguity.

To begin with I was finding my way in my new role. I had a tight grip on things and to a great extent controlled the staff. In fact, I was still doing too much myself at the start and had to learn to let go. For Arjan, this meant that he was told that he had a certain amount of freedom, only to be confronted with my development plans, training sessions and training methods.

At that moment it was what it was. Fortunately, we spoke about it openly and honestly, and we both agreed that Euro 2017 was the most important thing. After that, we'd have more time to evaluate our collaboration. From that moment on, I started to take more account of his input.

Vivianne Miedema, Leeuwinnen forward

Luckily, Sarina wasn't too proud to do everything on her own. She increasingly made a conscious choice to gather people around her whom she trusted and who complemented her. Foppe de Haan was chosen to assist her during Euro 2017. Sarina settled into her role as head coach quite swiftly. Once her team was put together, she could start working with us, and before long her focus shifted towards refining the team's tactics.

In Dutch football it's ingrained in our DNA to always play good football. In the months leading up to the Euros, that was our main focus. How would we build up our game when we had possession of the ball? How could we leverage our strengths both on and off the pitch? Our team had a lot of talent, and Sarina engaged in open conversations with us all, allowing the players to have their say too.

These conversations revolved around each player's contribution to the team. Each of us had specific qualities that we could use when we had possession of the ball. Sarina made us more aware of exactly what these qualities were, and we used them on the training pitch to establish a foundation for our matches. Despite the limited preparation time that Sarina had, it worked very well. We became a stable team that was hard to beat and knew exactly how to exploit our opponents' weaknesses.

After our success with the Leeuwinnen, it became clear that being a head coach involved more than just coaching the team. There were media, marketing and commerce expectations as well, especially after our win at Euro 2017. So, it was time for me to adapt my partnership with Arjan for the following tournament.

Timing was a crucial factor and I chose not to rush things immediately following the Euros. Instead, we began the qualifying rounds for the 2019 World Cup in France. As the period progressed, it became clear that certain changes were necessary. Although my instinctive feeling was that I was taking a step back, I knew that such changes were essential. At the end of the qualifying phase, I promised myself that I would talk to Arjan. However, events didn't unfold as anticipated, as we failed to qualify directly. We had to wait until we played the four playoff games and, eventually, secured our qualification for the World Championship before we could have that conversation.

Looking back, it may have been better to have discussed things before the playoffs, but qualifying was still our main priority at the time. When we finally talked, a few months later at my office in Zeist, it would be one of the most unusual conversations I'd had as a coach.

It was a conversation filled with emotion, introspection, mutual respect, focus and a desire to develop together. Neither of us was afraid to unburden ourselves about what was needed for our development and what the tension points would be. Sometimes with a tear, but also with a smile, because that was what our partnership was based on.

Arjan Veurink, Leeuwinnen assistant coach

Our success at Euro 2017 brought a lot of changes, not only to the Leeuwinnen as a team but also to the players and staff. There was a lot more attention on us, which meant that a lot of commercial opportunities opened up, and the team became heavily marketed. We were also scouting around 40 players, which made our workload much heavier, and it soon became clear that Sarina and the coaching staff couldn't handle all these additional responsibilities on their own. I was curious whether Sarina could make the step from wanting to do or control everything herself to gathering people around her and empowering them to do that. From coach to manager.

The step that Sarina had to make, I needed too. Her personal growth would give me space for my own ongoing development, so we needed to make the transition together. During the qualifiers for the 2019 World Cup I urged Sarina to go along with these changes, otherwise I wouldn't be able to continue working with her.

It turned out to be one of the pivotal moments in my transition from coach to manager. It was nerve-wracking to express to Arjan right from the start of our conversation that I wanted things to be done differently, but I felt it was necessary for both Arjan and myself. It was remarkable that we were able to explore this together, and it became clear right away that any outcome of our discussion would have been acceptable. It could have even led to us parting ways and by accepting that as a potential outcome, it became a truly exceptional moment. We marked the renewal of our partnership at that moment, laying the foundation for a new phase of collaboration.

The disappointment of having to compete in the play-offs prior to the World Cup actually turned out to be a blessing. It gave us the opportunity to carefully analyse what went right and what could be improved, not just for the team, but also for the staff and our own partnership. I'd prepared what I needed to say, and I trusted Arjan as a person and a professional. That helped me let go of what I found most exciting, such as creating a yearly plan, organising training sessions, delegating tasks to assistants and scouting for players.

I knew that achieving everything I wanted would take time, but it was important for me to rediscover my value to the team and the staff. At first, it was difficult for me just to be an observer during training sessions rather than an active participant. But I gradually learned to let go and appreciate the value of simply watching. It allowed me to better respond to the main points of each training day, whereas before, as a coach, I focused more on the execution of training drills. Most importantly, Arjan and I had extensive discussions about football. He constantly asked for my perspective, and we talked about the opportunities and the impact on the technical aspects of the game.

During our conversation, I told Arjan that I wanted to give our revamped partnership a try. We had two training camps planned leading up to the 2019 World Cup, and we decided to use these sessions to test out the new aspects of our collaboration. After each training session we took a moment to reflect and make any necessary adjustments. Both of us quickly recognised the potential of these changes and felt the benefits of working together more closely. Letting go and changing our behaviour was not easy, but I'm grateful that I took that step at the right time.

11

LEADERSHIP AND INCLUSION

I'm a naturally curious person, and I always seek out different perspectives to help me learn and broaden my horizons. Over the past few years I've often been asked to give presentations to various organisations across different sectors. Being the national team coach is a job that never stops; there's always more to do than time allows, which means that I've got to carefully manage my presentation schedule. I've come to appreciate the value of sharing my story about women's football, my views on leadership and on the parallels between sports and the business world. I always prepare thoroughly for my presentations and try to understand the requirements of the audience to which I'm speaking. Through the questions I receive during my talks and the reactions afterward, I often discover new insights or ideas about team-building, leadership or inclusivity. I enjoy learning from others so I can apply it to my own journey.

My sister Diana and I often compared notes on our respective career struggles. She paved the way for women in a male-dominated environment as one of BMW's first female managers, facing issues that are all too familiar to me. It's striking how similar our experiences have been working in such environments and the tactics we've used to overcome hurdles. I hope that more women can assume leadership roles, break age-old patterns and become role models for others in their sectors.

INCLUSIVITY NEEDS MORE THAN WORDS

Inclusivity is not something that can be achieved simply by saying the right things. It requires meaningful actions and a strong commitment to making it a reality.

Annelien Bredenoord is the inaugural female rector magnificus of Erasmus University Rotterdam, a position never previously held by a woman in the institution's hundred-year-plus history. While the barriers in education have only recently been lifted for women, they are now undeniably and fully open.

Annelien Bredenoord, rector magnificus of Erasmus University Rotterdam

The inclusivity programme at Erasmus University is a comprehensive plan with a multi-million-pound budget that's aimed at addressing the institutional barriers within the university. This includes encouraging individuals from diverse backgrounds to apply for influential positions in faculty councils or the university council. It involves diversifying selection committees, recruitment and selection processes, language usage, and promoting inclusive education.

A school assigned its students to write about football coaches. In the assignment description, Foppe de Haan was mentioned as the coach of the Leeuwinnen. I found this truly baffling, and I thought about writing a letter to the school to correct this. But on another occasion something amazing happened. I was taking a course, and guess what? I saw a gigantic photo of myself, displayed as an example of a successful sports coach. Can you imagine how incredible that felt? It was like a dream come true and a big step towards achieving a better balance in the sports world.

Annelien Bredenoord, rector magnificus of Erasmus University Rotterdam

True inclusivity isn't just about empty words or statements on paper. It's about taking action and making a real difference. Finally, we're seeing some positive changes happening. In the Netherlands, approximately one-third of university rectors are women. However, when it comes to professors, the numbers vary. There has been some improvement, but at my own institution, for example, only a quarter of professors are currently women. Research shows that around 30 per cent is the critical point for meaningful change. So, we haven't reached that level yet in the education sector, and it certainly shouldn't be our ultimate goal either. Why settle for just 30 per cent? It's a starting point to achieve a more balanced and inclusive environment. This example specifically addresses gender inclusivity, but there's still a long way to go.

The goal of having 30 per cent of important positions across different types of football organisations being occupied by women is still far distant. The FA and the KNVB are actively involved in addressing this issue, but it will take time before we see real progress. It is crucial for a sector to feel a strong sense of urgency for change. Corinne Vigreux, a French entrepreneur and co-founder of TomTom, as well as the founder of the Codam Coding

College, highlights the significant challenges that arise when women are not present in the tech industry.

Corinne Vigreux, co-founder of TomTom and founder of Codam

All across the tech industry, especially in higher management positions, it's mostly men who hold the jobs. We need women to show young people that they can achieve the same. They can explain why the tech sector is so fascinating and why it's crucial for women to navigate through the world of technology. Everyone uses technology every day, all year round, and there's no valid reason why women can't be a part of it. Technology plays an increasingly important role in every profession – just take a look at the latest advances in artificial intelligence – so we've no other option but to provide education for everyone.

I've always made an effort to motivate talented young female players and coaches to pursue careers in professional sports, as it's crucial to create opportunities for young women in all fields. In Western Europe, for instance, girls tend to focus on studying languages, while boys lean towards subjects like maths and engineering. Thankfully, this balance is more equitable in other parts of the world.

Corinne Vigreux, co-founder of TomTom and founder of Codam

There's no scientific evidence supporting the notion that girls or boys are inherently predisposed to excel in different academic areas. That they seem to do so is more a result of cultural influences in our society, which is truly disheartening. I established a computer training programme and recently had a conversation with a young woman who was studying at art school. She chose that path because she'd been repeatedly told that maths was not her strong suit, despite her lifelong fascination with the subject. She became disillusioned during her time at art school, however, and paid me a visit at Codam, an institute that offers programming education to everyone. She made the decision to give it a try, and she excelled in the initial phase of her programming training, being among the fastest learners. Remarkably, she completed the course in just 18 months, an impressive feat. Now she's returning to pursue studies in artificial intelligence, the most challenging field, and she's also doing a degree in maths.

This young woman had been influenced from a young age to believe that her talent lay in drawing, leading her to choose the art school path. It's only now, as an adult, that she's finally had the chance to discover her true aptitude for maths. She's now embarking on a journey that will have a significant impact on the world, with her AI studies opening doors to new possibilities.

All of this means that we must make more effort to provide opportunities for women. Opening up a sector and making it accessible to women requires a great deal of effort, as Elanor Boekholt-O'Sullivan explains. Born in Ireland, she made history in 2022 by becoming the first female lieutenant-general in the Dutch armed forces.

Elanor Boekholt-O'Sullivan, lieutenant-general in the Dutch armed forces

Around 30 per cent of civilian roles within the defence sector are currently occupied by women, but within the armed forces itself this figure declines sharply to an estimated 11 to 12 per cent. This stark contrast makes us question our efforts in the recruitment process. Women often seek the assurance that they possess the necessary skills before pursuing a career in the military, so we must intensify our initiatives to actively seek out and attract talented women. We openly encourage women to apply, recognising that the application process alone can enhance their self-confidence, irrespective of its outcome.

To promote inclusivity, I always ensure that there's female representation on selection committees. Leveraging my long tenure and wide networks within the military, I frequently introduce names of exceptional women that others may overlook. This strategy challenges our collective perspective and fosters a culture of diversity, empowering women to join the ranks of the defence sector.

I sometimes receive enquiries from women wondering why I've mentioned their names. In response, I tell them that they've already gained the necessary qualifications or have the potential to quickly acquire them. Sometimes, practical obstacles are raised that impede their ability to apply. In such cases we talk about the possibility of flexible application timelines or working collaboratively to eliminate barriers.

Opening doors for young women also involves making extra efforts to communicate with women who are otherwise difficult to reach. This is also a focus at Erasmus University.

Annelien Bredenoord, rector magnificus of Erasmus University Rotterdam

We dedicate a significant amount of time to visiting neighbourhoods in Rotterdam where going to university is less common. People feel apprehensive about stepping foot on the campus. It's intimidating and they believe it's not meant for them. That's why we're committed to opening the doors of the university, showing them that there are individuals just like them that have walked this path before and can serve as role models for aspiring students who are still unsure. The doors are already open for 12-year-old school students. We place great emphasis on creating positive experiences for young people at the university, even before they start their studies. Every summer we kick off a 'pre-academic programme' to prepare students who might find the prospect of studying daunting, helping them approach their journey with greater self-assurance.

Giving children opportunities to pursue their interests at a young age is crucial. I have personally experienced obstacles in playing football, but with the support of my parents I never let these hold me back. I am glad to see that progress is being made. By breaking down gender stereotypes early on, boys and girls can reach their full potential, and I wholeheartedly support this.

Corinne Vigreux, co-founder of TomTom and founder of Codam

Inclusive education means that children at a young age are not put in boxes. Persistent biases and stereotypes limit the potential of many individuals. Personally, I was raised to understand the importance of school and education in achieving success. I excelled in mathematics and physics. To break free from this narrow mindset, I moved to England after completing my studies when I was 22. Despite not speaking much English at the time, I didn't let that hold me back. My work then took me all across Europe. What helped me was my curiosity about different countries and the people I met. Through extensive travel, no one could pigeonhole me.

With Codam, our educational institute, we aim to empower as many people as possible in digital literacy. It's a college, but far from a conventional one. Codam provides everyone with an opportunity to study programming. Students from diverse backgrounds and of all genders find their place there, and many of them never believed they could do it. Currently, at least one-third of our students are women, and my goal is to reach 50 per cent in the future.

If I had the power, I'd introduce digital literacy into the school curriculum for young children, regardless of gender. Additionally, I'd transform education to prioritise creativity and emotions. The current focus on answers and grades disregards creativity. I'd encourage discovering different ways to solve problems and instil in children from a young age the courage to make mistakes.

THE DEMANDS AND REWARDS OF BEING A ROLE MODEL

I'm aware that I'm a role model for girls and women in football. Over the past few years the Lionesses and I have been able to give women's football a tremendous boost. The younger generation now see that they can become players or coaches at the highest level, and the achievements of individual players and teams greatly contribute to this. After every tournament in recent years, especially when first the Leeuwinnen and then the Lionesses became European champions, I saw the impact in the reactions of the younger generation, the new Liekes, Beths and Viviannes. It's a wonderful development and much needed, because every industry ought to have its role models for inclusivity.

Annelien Bredenoord, rector magnificus of Erasmus University Rotterdam

My first impression of Sarina was that she's a role model because she exudes a combination of vulnerability and toughness. That's the image that stands out for me. Role models are often seen as pioneers. But I always stress that many people can be role models. Leadership isn't just about

271

one hierarchical leader or the person who's always in the spotlight. It's about all of us. I see Sarina as a true pioneer who goes against the grain to do what she loves: play football. I know she was creative with the rules from the start, like cutting her hair short. Maybe she already knew where she was going and what her destiny was, even if it was subconscious. When you achieve something by going against the norm, you inspire a lot of people. Not just a new generation, but especially your own generation. The people I know are encouraged and inspired by what Sarina has achieved.

The more tournaments I coach, the more requests flood in for interviews, lectures, presentations and sometimes even talks at schools. Unfortunately, I have to decline the vast majority of them. My schedule doesn't allow for it, as there's always a new qualifying round or tournament to prepare for. I've long wondered who actually wants to go to my presentations. Now, I 'understand' that a bit better, because of the consecutive successes in recent years. Through the feedback I've received, I know that people are genuinely interested in me and often draw inspiration from what I've been a part of. But it's easier for others to see you as a role model than for yourself to do so. And many role models have already experienced in their youth the feeling that nothing can stop them from doing what they love most. That's certainly the case for me.

Annelien Bredenoord, rector magnificus of Erasmus University Rotterdam

At a young age I already knew that I held ethics in high regard and wanted to actively engage in politics. I decided to study theology, an unconventional choice that raised many questions and even surprised some people. My intuition that it was right for me was strong enough that I stuck with the subject, and I combined it with the study of political science, becoming active in the Dutch social liberal political party D66 while also being a member of a traditional student association. In the end, it worked out well.

At a young age, I also realised that I might be attracted to women. My parents supported me and encouraged me to explore it. Only by exploring it can you truly understand what it means for you. This was important to me because I felt different at school. I thought I was the only one. As a 15-year-old I didn't know anyone who was open about it. It was only after I went to university that I came into contact with more people who were open about their sexuality. Sometimes, my mother would mention to people that I liked women, and they would respond with, 'Oh, I'm so sorry.' My mother would then express her confusion because I wasn't dead. She'd come home and tell me about it, and we'd have a good laugh together.

Nowadays, I give a few lectures or presentations each year, discussing my career path and/or the achievements of the teams I coach. I have less and less stage fright, and I now know what I want to say. But being a role model is also uncomfortable. It drains my energy because I'm not naturally someone who enjoys being in the spotlight. However, when I'm on stage these days or when I see the cameras pointing at me during a press conference, I feel the power of the bigger mission. For years, others have emphasised the importance of having someone who shows that it is possible to be a female coach. That mission is important, so I fully commit to it, despite my innate timidity.

Elanor Boekholt-O'Sullivan, lieutenant-general in the Dutch armed forces

When I think of Sarina, I think of her incredible achievements, both nationally and internationally, and the way she has put girls, women and football on the map. I admire how she has broken into an industry dominated by men and made it accessible to women. No one has done it like her before. Of course, a man can say that women's football is a great sport, but it's so much more powerful when a woman says it and is successful in it. Girls who see her know that they can maybe achieve it too. It's necessary for a woman to be there and speak up.

Sarina's modesty truly expresses her personality, but the fact that she's a role model is more important than her own discomfort about it. Over the years I've started thinking differently about this. As you get older and experience the impact of your actions, you realise how important it is. I'm very good at saying these things about others, but I feel the same discomfort when it comes to myself. I score highly on introversion – I don't really want to speak in public, I don't like being on a stage. But if I don't do it, if I don't speak up about how important these matter are, then I'm letting down many people, including women who are not considering joining or staying in the armed forces. It's impossible to be an invisible role model.

WHAT DOES IT TAKE?

Achieving inclusivity requires a lot. Not just from the role models in different industries, but from everyone. Whether in sports or in the business world, you should be able to be yourself. With the Leeuwinnen and the Lionesses, I spent a lot of time creating a psychologically safe environment for the team, one that allows us to make mistakes and grow as individuals and as a team. It inevitably comes with ups and downs, but it's the right thing to do. For example, in preparation for the 2023 World Cup, it was incredibly disappointing that we lost the friendly against Australia, but ultimately it was also good as we were able to use that experience to evaluate and improve our performance. As strange as it may sound, I'm a strong advocate of making mistakes. It means that you've committed yourself to doing something. It might be successful or it might fail, but you always learn from it. And that's what it's all about – growth. Of course, it's different if someone keeps making the same mistake and doesn't develop further.

Corinne Vigreux, co-founder of TomTom and founder of Codam

Making mistakes is allowed! It's crucial to create moments for learning, but this can only happen in a safe place. In that environment a team can try new things, which is especially important in the tech field. If you don't make mistakes, then you haven't tried hard enough.

As a team we value both the success and the failure of actions. The team is the most important aspect. Just like in sports, all the facilities and conditions can be the same, but the quality of the team determines real success. We select the right individuals, motivate them and show them what success looks like, letting them taste success. And when things go wrong, we make sure that everyone feels safe and knows that there won't be any backlash. I'm always the first to acknowledge that mistakes are learning moments. We pause only briefly, in order to keep moving forward. It's all about good teamwork.

Being allowed to make mistakes means that I encourage the players and staff to voice their opinions when asked, preferably without considering the fact that I'm the coach. Ultimately, I'm just part of the team, and I value the opinion of every player or staff member equally. When I started in England, we initially needed time to gain everyone's trust, to let our safe working environment do its thing. Since the staff and players feel the trust, they realise that making mistakes is part of our culture and that opinions can be given without any judgement. This way, the discussions between all of us have become more open.

Elanor Boekholt-O'Sullivan, lieutenant-general in the Dutch armed forces

I find it difficult when I have an idea that I'm not completely sure about. I want to be able to talk about it with the team, but sometimes it's tough. Because of my position, my opinion sometimes carries more weight and other people might quickly go along with it because they think that's what the general wants. I had to get used to that.

I often delay giving my own opinion to harness the power of the team. I achieved this mainly by investing in the people I work closely with – selecting the right individuals for my team, taking great care in the relationship between us and encouraging them from the beginning to keep me sharp. And then by repeating that message. I also want to be accessible to my people, so everything in my room has a purpose. An inviting round table is there so we can have discussions together and the photo wall displays pictures of all the staff, which draws people like a magnet. It's all designed to remove barriers that may be experienced within the strict hierarchy of the Ministry of Defence.

As a role model, it's important to be accessible to your team, and I've invested a lot of time in this since the beginning of my coaching career. There are various ways you can encourage this accessibility. If a player needs me or the staff, they can always come to us. They know how to reach me, and when a question comes up I give my full attention to that person. I've learned that real attention starts with making time and listening well. As a result, I think the players are less hesitant to approach me. Despite my best efforts, however, in England I'm still occasionally told that I'm quite direct, sometimes too direct. The Netherlands and England: two countries that are so close to each other, yet so different. I'm curious about how my directness would be experienced in other cultures.

Corinne Vigreux, co-founder of TomTom and founder of Codam

Of course, I take cultural differences into consideration when travelling in a different country. Particularly when I visit a different continent such as Asia, I have a different approach and pay attention to my body language. I research the cultural norms of a country beforehand and try to align myself with them as best I can. I strive to understand the people I am with to the best of my ability. My curiosity often comes in handy. If any sensitivities arise, I try to resolve them myself by questioning what I can do differently. Explaining the reasons behind my decisions also helps: explaining why I do things the way I do.

In other industries, showing vulnerability is often a breakthrough moment to being your true self. It's part of being allowed to make mistakes, acknowledging that something is difficult and having the courage to speak about it out loud. Unfortunately, this is not yet commonplace everywhere and there's still a lot of progress to be made in this area.

Elanor Boekholt-O'Sullivan, lieutenant-general in the Dutch armed forces

I chaired a NATO conference on the importance of women on missions and delivered a speech to the cadets of the Royal Military Academy about mental health. In doing so, I addressed both men and women but with a slightly stronger emphasis on women, to let them know that they too can become generals. Showing vulnerability is becoming increasingly important in the military, and I mentioned this to the cadets by opening up and sharing what goes through my mind when people ask me how I'm doing. In truth, I can't really answer that question. What exactly does someone mean? Physically or mentally? Do they genuinely want to know?

At one point, as I looked around, I saw several cadets with tears in their eyes. This made me uncomfortable, but I also knew that my comments hadn't been in vain. I'd succeeded in raising the profile of vulnerability for men and women, as well as offering women an optimistic perspective as to what the military might hold for them, both collectively and on an individual level. Together with others, I'm trying to ensure there's a better transition towards inclusivity in the armed forces, a better balance between masculinity and showing vulnerability, and more room for differences in personality, both introverted and extroverted.

In the air force, you can be a skilled pilot even if you have reserved character. I've now reached a position in the military where I determine which topics are discussed, and I've become better at explicitly expressing my moral compass in conversations, without questioning whether it will be appreciated or not.

Inclusivity and leadership are vitally important topics, especially in football. It's remarkable to see how many similarities there are with other sectors and industries. There's still a lot of work to be done in every profession to improve opportunities for girls and women. That's why I always feel delighted to see role models fighting for this cause and taking risks, including the Lionesses and the Leeuwinnen. I now also recognise the power of my own fame and am prepared to take on that responsibility, even if it means facing discomfort at times. In fact I willingly embrace it.

12

REACHING NEW HEIGHTS IN AUSTRALIA

The 2023 Women's World Cup in Australia and New Zealand was the largest one yet. FIFA decided to expand the tournament to include 32 teams, eight more than in the previous edition. Initially, I had some doubts, fearing that there might be some lopsided matches, like the 13–0 victory by the United States over Thailand in 2019. However, now that the tournament is over, I can confidently say that FIFA made the right choice. The expansion served as a catalyst for the participating nations, giving the signal that women's football is significant worldwide. Fans from 32 countries were treated to an amazing summer of sport. The tournament showcased impressive talent and featured thrilling matches, with teams from all corners of the globe leaving their mark.

Right from the start we faced a strong contender from another continent, Haiti, in our first game of the group stage. We'd analysed their previous matches carefully to prepare ourselves, but since we'd never played against them before it was difficult to gauge their true strength. We knew they had exceptional athletes, a well-organised defence and posed a threat on the counter. Their midfielder Melchie Dumornay was particularly dangerous. Overall, Haiti were tricky opponents for our opening game.

Before the World Cup we made a deliberate choice not to travel to other continents for friendly matches. While it would have been ideal to play against teams from different parts of the world, the disruption from all the travel would have been overwhelming. The fixture list our players had to handle was already packed, and it didn't make sense to add further journeys across multiple time zones for friendlies – we prioritised the well-being of our players over everything else. However, we were genuinely intrigued by Haiti's strengths and capabilities. As the referee blew the whistle, our highly anticipated opening game in Brisbane finally began.

Opening matches are often difficult. I was really interested to see how our team would handle the match, as we knew we had to improve as the tournament progressed. Before the World Cup started our players had a two-week break after their end of their domestic leagues, then trained individually for a week to recover from the physical demands of the season. This build-up phase meant we needed some time to reach peak performance. It was crucial to get defender Millie Bright back in shape after Leah Williamson had to drop out due to an injury. Millie hadn't played since April and had been putting in lots of hard work to regain her fitness and form for the World Cup. The rhythm of the group stage matches would help both her and the rest of the team reach the level of performance necessary to go far in the tournament.

The match against Haiti turned out to be a challenging opening game, as they often are in tournaments. Fortunately, we were awarded a penalty in the first half, which Georgia Stanway converted. We had opportunities to score a second goal later in the game, but our possession was sometimes sloppy. Haiti came out quick and threatening several times, forcing Mary Earps to make a fantastic save towards the final whistle to secure our victory by a single goal.

ADJUSTING THE GAME PLAN AGAINST DENMARK

In our second group game we faced Denmark, a team we were fairly familiar with. We were aware of their strengths and knew the best way to play against them. Both the coaching staff and the team agreed that we had to step up our game from the previous match. We made two changes to the starting line-up. We had different options for our defence – if we wanted to prioritise defending we chose Jess Carter in the centre, but if we leaned towards attacking we favoured Alex Greenwood. For the game against Denmark in Sydney we decided to start with Alex, and we opted for Lauren James in attack.

The first half of the match went really well for us, at least until the 38th minute. Lauren James scored an incredible goal just six minutes into the game, but seven minutes before half-time midfielder Keira Walsh had to be carried off the field with what seemed like a serious injury. Despite our readiness for such scenarios, it soon became evident that Keira's absence was impacting on the team's performance. We'd already lost key players to serious injuries earlier in the season, and it made us wonder when this streak of bad luck would end.

After Keira was substituted our performance became less confident. In the end it was Lauren James's goal that gave us the winning edge, earning us three points once again. As soon as the game ended we spoke to the medical staff to get an update on Keira's injury. We refrained from speculation, knowing that the outside world would be doing enough of that already. Our experienced medical team concluded that an MRI scan was necessary to determine the exact nature of the injury, and although their initial assessment suggested that it might not be as severe as it first appeared, we decided to withhold any official communication until we had more clarity. It was crucial for Keira to understand the problem before making any announcements. Fortunately, when the MRI scan came through we were told that there was a good chance she could continue playing as the tournament progressed. This news brought a much-needed boost and relief to both Keira and the team, but to avoid speculation about her recovery timeline we only disclosed that it wasn't a cruciate ligament injury.

We'd already faced numerous challenges with the team, but Keira's injury had an impact on both the players and the flow of the game against Denmark. However, we knew that the Lionesses possessed incredible resilience in the face of adversity and we believed we could overcome this challenge as well. I was proud that we managed to maintain our lead and secure a victory in our second group game. Yet something was still bothering me.

Although we'd already accumulated six points from two games, I'd a feeling that we needed to make some sort of change. If we simply continued on the same path, we'd just keep getting the same results. The question was whether that would be enough to achieve our dream with the team. The morning after our game against Denmark, Arjan and I sat down for coffee and discussed our thoughts on the first two games. Arjan quickly suggested that this was the perfect time to start with a different formation. I fully supported his idea and knew we had to discuss it with the rest of the staff as soon as possible.

We'd actually talked about this during the preparations for the World Cup. In April 2023 we'd discussed the possibility of setting ourselves up differently, with a goalkeeper, three central defenders, two wing-backs, three midfielders and two strikers. This formation, also known as a 3–5–2, seemed promising. However, due to a few factors such as fewer injuries and a slightly different squad make-up at the time, we'd never had the chance to extensively practise it. Instead, we focused on other strategies such as building attacks from the back with four or three defenders, utilising wing play and attacking around the opponent's penalty area. With limited time to work with the national squad, choices had to be made regarding which patterns of play to drill.

As a coach, I always emphasise the importance of training and practising new formations before they're implemented in match situations. For a tournament, it's crucial to prepare for all possible scenarios and ensure that the players know their roles within the game plan. Unfortunately, we didn't have the luxury of time to do so on this occasion, but we still decided to make the change.

It was immediately apparent that the technical staff was convinced that we needed to apply the formation change, and while the injury to Keira Walsh was certainly a factor to consider, we'd have made the same decision even if she hadn't been injured. Before we discussed this with the leading group of players, we had to make sure everything was in place and transparent. During the tournament, we realised that we needed a change, and we were ready to make it happen. Additionally, we had enough time and space to do so since we had already prepared for other scenarios. Moreover, many of our players had prior experience playing in this formation for their clubs, which would make the transition smoother.

Just like the coaching staff, the leading group of players responded with excitement when we presented them with our plan. They understood the reasoning behind it and saw the potential benefits it would bring. The 3–5–2 formation relies heavily on having two wing backs who can execute the plan effectively, and we were fortunate to have Lucy Bronze and Rachel Daly, who had the skills to do so. Furthermore, we had a squad with versatile players who could excel in many different positions, which was crucial when making substitutions. The final group game against China was the perfect opportunity to implement this new game plan. With two wins already under our belt, we were in a strong position to advance to the last

16, and we knew that our rejigged formation would pose a challenge to China.

Right from the start the players were able to find each other easily in this new set-up, and Alessia Russo scored a goal just four minutes into the game, giving the team even more confidence, with Lauren Hemp adding a second, making it 2–0.

Throughout my years as a national coach, I've had the privilege of working with incredible talent. It brings me immense joy to support their growth as elite athletes and that always comes with peaks and troughs. In the first group game against Haiti, Lauren James made a significant impact as a substitute, then scored the only goal against Denmark, and now she was having an outstanding performance against China. The result was a remarkable 6–1 victory, and it was truly fantastic to see her contribute so greatly to the team with two goals and three assists.

Tournaments like this are incredibly intense both for me and the coaching staff. What really energises me is seeing the players grow and develop, knowing how much effort they put in to fulfil their ambitions. In the game against China I decided to include Katie Zelem in the starting line-up. I believe she's a smart player and a valued member of the team both on and off the field. Back in April I didn't pick her for the squad because I wanted to try some different things in her position, but when I finally decided to bring her into the World Cup squad I noticed a change. She'd previously told me that she used to focus intently on following my instructions to a tee, but now she was playing with much more freedom. I encouraged her to continue developing in this way, and she excelled in the position, especially after Keira Walsh had suffered her injury. She had a fantastic game against China, and I couldn't help but enjoy watching her.

The success we achieved with this new formation reassured the staff that we'd made the right decision. It was thrilling to see it work so well against China, as we knew they would be a tough team to face. The energy and enthusiasm we'd witnessed during training with the leading group of players translated onto the field. This gave us great hope for the next phase of the tournament, as every game from now on was in a knock-out format.

PLAYING WITH PASSION

Our opponents in the round of 16 were Nigeria. We'd already recognised the strength of teams from different continents in the tournament, and Nigeria were no exception. In the group stage they'd played two goalless draws, and won against the tournament co-hosts Australia. This meant we were up against tough opponents who were hard to score against.

The game was full of high-energy tension and drama for me, as there was so much happening on the field. Usually, I can stay focused and analyse the game calmly, assessing what's going well and what needs improvement. We were evenly matched. Both Nigeria and the Lionesses had good opportunities to score, but the match remained goalless. However, just before full-time Lauren James received a red card for a foul on her opponent. Things can happen in the heat of the battle that are difficult to explain, and Lauren found herself in such a moment. This was undoubtedly really tough for her and the entire team, especially considering the high she'd experienced in the previous game against China.

My first concern was to ensure that our team's organisation didn't suffer after the sending-off. The moment there was a VAR check for a possible red card, I immediately called some of the players over to the touchline and ran through the tactics that we'd prepared in case of such an event. During moments like these I'm completely focused and willing to do anything to strengthen the way the team is set up as quickly as possible. My husband Marten told me after the match that I'd given Lauren Hemp a push to hurry her up and get her to the other side of the field. I hadn't even realised it at the time, but of course I apologised to her after the match and we shared a good laugh about it.

I also realised straight away that it might not necessarily be in Nigeria's favour to play against ten women as they weren't used to taking control of the game themselves. Up until that point they'd been creating chances by defending well, then making quick transitions when they regained possession. I had full confidence that we'd make it through extra-time without conceding and had a sense that the outcome would be decided through a penalty shoot-out.

I've a clear vision when it comes to shoot-outs. Our technical staff are well prepared and organised when it comes to the planning and executing of penalty kicks. Darren Ward and Kate Hays take the lead in this, ensuring that each player has their own plan, and Darren has worked closely with the goalkeepers on how to save the opposition's shots.

Taking a penalty under the gaze of tens of thousands of passionate fans in a packed stadium is an entirely different ballgame from slotting one in on the practice pitch. It's all about experience and coping with the pressure. Thankfully, we'd already had that penalty shoot-out against Brazil at Wembley Stadium in front of more than 80,000 people. Many of our players are also the designated penalty takers for their respective clubs, where they often perform before large crowds.

When it comes to penalty kicks, we make all the necessary preparations with the staff before the game begins. We create a list with all 23 players on the squad and decide on the order in which the penalties will be taken. During the game against Nigeria that list was narrowed down to 10 players, and just before the end of extra-time Arjan Veurink and Darren Ward, the goalkeeping coach, showed me the finalised list. This moment had already been planned before the game, so it all happened very quickly. Arjan then went to each player with the list, explaining the proposed sequence of penalty takers. While there may be preferences from some players for a different order, against Nigeria we stuck to the original sequence.

The last phase is – as always – the execution of the plan. Since the players have extensively practised various penalty-taking techniques, their chances of scoring increase significantly. This preparation paid off and we went through 4–2 on penalties.

Following the game against Nigeria, we received news that Lauren James would be banned for two matches due to her red card. This meant that she'd miss both the quarter-final against Colombia and the semi-final, should we reach that stage. It was a tough setback for her and understandably affected her deeply. As a team, we tried to give her as much support as possible. Our priority was to discuss the situation calmly, finding a balance between it being a learning experience and providing encouragement to help her move on. Moments like these highlight how crucial our care for each other is for the squad.

Additionally, our communications team kept a close eye on media coverage and social media responses following the game and the red card incident. As players and staff we try not to pay too much attention to outside noise, preferring to direct our energy towards our performances, but the comms team will inform us about specific reactions, good or bad, if they feel it's really necessary. It's generally only after the tournament – when our friends and family share their stories with us – that we hear about what's been said in the media.

Unfortunately, in football, including women's football, we're increasingly having to deal with anonymous online hate and racism towards both players and staff. I have personally witnessed the impact of this on both the Leeuwinnen and the Lionesses. Posting abusive material under the cloak of anonymity is cowardly and reprehensible behaviour, and I hope that we can find a way of dealing with it in the future.

Despite these challenges, we managed to focus on our next game: the quarter-final against Colombia. Before the game kicked off I was struck by the passion shown by the Colombian players and their many fans as they sang their national anthem. When we played at home in the Euros a year ago we were motivated by the support of tens of thousands of fans. However, in Australia, the situation was different. Due to distance and costs, this time there were far fewer England fans in attendance, and we were playing against teams whose passionate supporters outnumbered ours. It's incredible progress for stadiums to be filled to capacity for women's football. As a coach it's fantastic to be in a sold-out stadium, even if most of the spectators are cheering for the opposition. You simply can't compare the energy created by a huge crowd to a match where most seats are empty.

The Colombian team also demonstrated their passion during the game. By this point in the tournament we'd found our stride, displaying our adaptability and resilience during difficult moments. The change in formation that we'd made in the group stage was proving to be increasingly effective. However, just before half-time, we found ourselves trailing by a goal scored by their midfielder Leicy Santos. Going behind is when a team's experience truly shines. It's about staying composed, staying alert and executing the plan. We were fortunate when the Colombian goalkeeper fumbled the ball right before the break, allowing Lauren Hemp to poke home an equaliser, although it was in great part due to the relentless pressure that Alessia Russo and Lauren were putting on their goalkeeper. They seized every opportunity when there was even a slight chance of her losing control of the ball.

After half-time Alessia scored a second goal to seal the win 2–1, meaning we had a match-up with Australia, the co-hosts, who'd reached the semi-final by defeating France in a penalty shoot-out. Many of the so-called 'big' countries had already been eliminated: Germany, Brazil and Canada in the group stage, the reigning world champions, the United States, in the Round of 16, and the Netherlands in the quarter-finals. Now, there were only four teams left competing for the title: Spain, Sweden, Australia and us.

INTIMIDATION IS INSPIRATION

Even though our semi-final was against the same team who'd beaten us 2–0 in a friendly back in April, with Sam Kerr and Charlotte Grant scoring for the Matildas, we didn't once mention that match during our preparations. The situation we were currently in was so different that it was almost irrelevent. We did discuss the game when we gathered at the Lionesses' training camp in June, but that was the extent of it. We also decided not to use any video footage from our defeat, as we didn't want to provoke any negative memories among the players.

What we did consider was the fact that the stadium would be filled with over 80,000 enthusiastic Australian fans. We knew from our experience at Euro 2022 in England how much of a positive impact that could have on a team. This presented one of the biggest challenges for us in the semi-final: intimidation is inspiration. We firmly believed that we could defeat Australia, and we wanted to silence the crowd through our exceptional skills.

The game was scheduled for the evening of Wednesday 16 August, and ten minutes before kick-off I walked out of the players' tunnel onto the pitch with the rest of the staff. The semi-final was about to begin. With each step I took, the noise from the crowd in the stadium grew ever louder. Although most of the cheering was not for us, unlike at Wembley when we faced Germany in the Euros final, it was a positive thing for women's football that what we experienced a year earlier was now being reproduced in Australia.

As I took my place in the dugout and the players gathered in the tunnel ready to walk out into the stadium, I couldn't help but remember my days as a player myself. Back then, we were thrilled if five hundred people came to watch a match. It was mostly family, friends and a few supporters cheering us on. This tournament was proof that the massive crowds at Euro 2022 were no flash in the pan. Considering my own experiences as a player, this was something truly special.

As always, I made sure to stand closest to the players when they stepped onto the pitch. Maybe they don't think much of it, but I applaud them before every game. It feels great to be near them in that moment, to feel a connection and to show my support for them in the upcoming match. Tournaments can be intense for me too. I try to enjoy them more and more, but if I'm honest I still find it challenging. That's why the moment right before the game is so important to me. Sometimes, I've got to pause and appreciate just how special these moments truly are.

We got off to a good start in the game. We were now both accustomed to and confident in our 3–5–2 formation. Just as in the match against Colombia, our starting line-up in the attack consisted of Ella Toone, Lauren Hemp and Alessia Russo. Before halftime, Ella Toone scored an excellent goal, putting us 1–0 ahead with a shot into the right-hand corner. In the second half Sam Kerr, who was in the starting line-up for the first time in the tournament, proved once again how important she was for Australia, scoring a tremendous equaliser in the 63rd minute.

During that period we stuck to our game plan, which included playing long passes from the back to exploit the spaces that were opening up behind the Australian defense. Millie Bright executed this perfectly in the 71st minute, creating a difficult situation for the Australian back line. They couldn't handle it, and Lauren Hemp seized the opportunity, bundling one in to make it 2–1 for us.

Australia increased the pressure and had several chances in quick succession. However, we managed to intercept one of their attacks, and Lauren Hemp gained possession. Her well-timed pass to Alessia Russo enabled her to score our third goal.

We'd done it. We played an outstanding game against the co-hosts Australia, with 85,000 fans cheering them on, and secured our spot in the final. It was an incredible feeling!

WHO'LL PLAY THE BEST GAME?

Throughout our time in Australia we stayed in Terrigal, just north of Sydney. We were fortunate that all of our games, including the group stages, were played in Australia, although it was a shame that we never had the chance to visit New Zealand. The Australians did their best to make us feel welcome in Terrigal. It's crucial to have a comfortable and inspiring environment when you spend such a long time together as a team. The branding team at the FA had described it as our home away from home. The hotel was decorated with the Lionesses' values, including slogans such as 'Team first', 'Thrive in the moment' and 'Stick together', and photos of all of the players when they were young had been put up on the walls.

The FA planned everything to perfection. They provided a special bus for family and friends, who were mostly based near Sydney, to come and visit us at our hotel for family gatherings in the room that was set aside for meet-ups. We didn't have many of these during the tournament, but those few we did have made a significant impact, allowing us to share our experiences, be ourselves and hear news from outside the football bubble. Another benefit was that although Terrigal felt like it had been taken over by English fans, there were plenty of restaurants in the area where family and friends could spend time together undisturbed.

My husband Marten was able to join me in Australia for the entire tournament, and the moments we shared together were truly wonderful. They made me realise just how intense the tournament was, and it was so refreshing just to be able to relax with him, let go of all the pressures and be rejuvenated.

Our opponents in the final were Spain, who'd beaten Sweden. Being back in a final with the Lionesses once again, after leading them to their triumph in the Euros just a year earlier, made me realise just how incredible our journey had been. The expectations were sky-high in

England, but many teams in the World Cup had similar hopes from their home base, only for them to be dashed during the tournament. In the end, only Spain and us made it all the way to the final. I felt immense pride that we'd reached this far and had the opportunity to inspire England with our football once again. It was also a chance to show girls and boys what they could achieve if they aspired to greatness.

Reaching a final is never easy, but once you're there, winning becomes the goal. This mindset was evident in our preparations. Our coaching staff and I made sure to express how proud we were of the team and how they'd overcome all the challenges that had been thrown their way. But we also stressed how much we wanted to finish on a high note by defeating Spain, playing the best match we've ever played and fulfilling all our dreams. Spain had been exceptional throughout the tournament, with the exception of their game against Japan, where they showed some vulnerability. They were familiar opponents, as we'd faced them in the quarter-finals of Euro 2022 in England, ultimately beating them 2–1.

In contrast to that match against Spain at the Euros, we played the first half of the 2023 World Cup final, on Sunday 20 August, in our – now permanent – 3–5–2 formation. We knew that Spain would dominate possession, and that's exactly what happened. The first good chance fell to us, but unfortunately the ball struck the crossbar. We'd been hoping to score first to make the game easier for us, but we couldn't find the back of the net. Instead, it was Spain who took a 1–0 lead in the 29th minute.

Spain played their best game in the final, making it difficult for the Lionesses to put them under consistent pressure. Whenever we did manage to create a chance, they dealt with it brilliantly. At half-time, we made some changes, switching back to our original 4–3–3 formation from the group stage. This meant making two substitutions so we had three attackers on the field, with Lauren James and Chloe Kelly coming on right at the start of the second half. This proved effective in the first 15 minutes after the break, as we looked dangerous in front of the goal.

However, everything changed in the 69th minute when the referee awarded a penalty to Spain after a VAR check. VAR took forever to make a decision, and it disrupted the flow of the game, but Mary Earps kept us in it with an outstanding save and gave the team a huge boost. At that point I firmly believed that the match was still up for grabs.

However, what made matters worse was our inability to regain our rhythm in the final part of the match. In addition to that incredibly long VAR delay, Alex Greenwood got injured and play had to be stopped for several minutes. We knew this would result in a significant amount of injury time, and we were right – there were an extra 13 minutes added on. Just before the end of regular time we adopted a strategy that had worked well for us the previous year against the same opponents. Millie Bright moved up into an attacking position, and we tried to create scoring opportunities by playing long balls towards her.

Unfortunately, we were unable to play enough long balls up to our strikers as Spain really started pressing, making it difficult to execute those passes at the right moments. Despite our best efforts we couldn't find an equaliser, and Spain held on to their 1–0 lead to become world champions. Losing a final is always painful, but I genuinely offer my congratulations to Spain on their well-deserved win. They played their best game when it mattered most, and on this occasion we fell just short.

After the match I made sure to express the immense pride I felt for the team, especially considering the problems we'd faced both before and during the tournament. I'm incredibly proud of how the players stepped up, how they adapted to different formations and how they showed resilience throughout. My hope is that our performance in Australia can serve as inspiration for all the girls and women who share our love for the game, and that it paves the way for greater opportunities in their playing and coaching careers. *This is just the beginning!*

EPILOGUE

In recent years I've been a head coach for national teams, and that really has a different dynamic to working as a club coach. I've had the opportunity to do both, and I enjoy them equally. The intensity is similar, but the way it's expressed is different.

When you're a club coach, you're on the pitch with your team every day. You've got more opportunity to try new things during practice, and more time to work with your staff and players to perfect your style of play and your teamwork. As a national team head coach you don't get to spend as much time with your players, so you can't afford to have bad training sessions. When the players are with their clubs, we focus on scheduling training camps and I obviously have much less contact with the players. There are around 40 players that we monitor at their clubs to see how they're performing, and when they're not with the national team I'm able to work from different locations.

Right now, I haven't decided if I want to continue being a national team head coach or switch to being a club coach. But what I do know is that I want to work at the highest level. I won't make any compromises when it comes to that. I really enjoy my work at the FA, where we operate at the top level, and I believe in staying loyal and building something meaningful wherever I'm employed.

In my journey of making important choices, my family has always been a crucial factor. When I was coaching at ADO Den Haag, it was both enjoyable and incredibly demanding. The intensity eventually took its toll, leading to illness. That experience taught me the importance of maintaining a healthy work–life balance.

Moving to the KNVB brought me greater stability. Since then, my husband Marten and I have made decisions together, and we always consider how they will affect our family. Being there for each other and for our children is of utmost importance to me. Transitioning from club coach to national team head coach aligned well with our family dynamic. Marten consistently supported my development and was able to take care of things at home when needed. He said, 'Sarina, you've been a true professional for years, and now you have the opportunity to turn it into your actual job. Go for it, and we will figure it out together.' I wish every woman had such support from her family, especially during the challenging phase of raising young children.

Our decision to join the Lionesses was also a joint one. We anticipated greater press interest and the bigger scale of the job in England, and the fact that I'd be working abroad was a new adventure. While certain elements remained the same as being head coach of the Leeuwinnen, these were important factors to consider, such as the pressure of being away from home for two months with the Lionesses during the summer due to tournaments. This was the case with the Leeuwinnen in 2017 (European Championship), 2019 (World Cup), and ultimately in 2021 (with the Olympic Games being postponed by a year due to the pandemic). And this pattern would continue with the Lionesses, as we had the European Championship in 2022 and the World Cup in 2023.

For me, that can only work if Marten and our children are up for it. Our family situation is changing and there will come a time when our daughters will no longer live at home. That will have a different impact. But one thing will remain constant: in any future decision, it's important for me to consider all the pros and cons together with Marten.

People often wonder if a female coach can lead a men's team. This question does a disservice to women. Of course a woman can coach a men's team. It's absurd to even question or debate this, just like it's absurd to question if a man can coach a women's team.

I hope we can keep inspiring everybody – girls, women, boys and men – to go play football. The love of football brings people together. It's crucial for the future of the game that women have more visibility. Just like what we tell the players during the World Cup, I want to tell you as the reader: take action! Don't let anyone stop or discourage you, just go for it, because you can. Believe in yourself and don't be afraid of making mistakes, because mistakes are part of your growth. Mistakes don't mean you're not good enough. It means you're evolving. You will become the best version of yourself.

At the time of writing this, the next women's world championship will take place in 2027. We have a four-year window to ensure that all the top players in the world are in peak physical condition and have the opportunity to showcase their skills. Four years for research and development across various aspects of youth and women's football. Hopefully, over the course of these four years, we can make the necessary investments and advancements to foster the growth of women's football in all areas.

Across every continent and in every country giving girls and women the opportunity to participate in football, in any role at any level. That's my dream!

ACKNOWLEDGEMENTS

SARINA AND JEROEN

We're incredibly grateful for the support and enthusiasm we have received from so many people in writing this book. The conversations we've had with each other and with others were so beautiful, so open, that they inspired us to bring that strength and vulnerability to the pages of *What It Takes*.

The FA and the KNVB have been involved and supportive right from the beginning, helping us capture the key moments of the Lionesses and the Leeuwinnen through words and photographs. Thank you, Mark Bullingham and Jan Dirk van der Zee, for your support.

This book also exists thanks to all the players, staff members, administrators, fellow coaches and others who generously shared their experiences without hesitation.

Elanor Boekholt-O'Sullivan, Annelien Bredenoord, Millie Bright, Lucy Bronze, Sue Campbell, Merel van Dongen, Mary Earps, Louis van Gaal, David Gerty, Anja van Ginhoven, Kate Hays, Nigel de Jong, Lieke Martens, Beth Mead, Vivianne Miedema, Lennard van Ruiven, Jill Scott, Geraint Twose, Arjan Veurink, Corinne Vigreux, Ellen White and Leah Williamson: thank you so much for your candid conversations.

Last but not least, a big thank you to Erwin Koning and Rose Sandy from our publisher HarperCollins in the Netherlands and the UK. This book truly is a team effort!

SARINA

Without my management, Pauline Siemers and Lienke van Santvoort, I wouldn't have been able to write this book. In the foreground and behind the scenes, you worked tirelessly to keep everything manageable for me. What amazing teamwork.

Jeroen, thank you so much for the countless conversations we've had and the way the information has made its way into the book.

Above all, I want to thank Marten, Sacha, Lauren, my father and mother (†), my parents-in-law and my twin brother Tom and sister Diana (†) for the unwavering support I've always received and felt. Thank you!

JEROEN

Sarina, thank you for confiding in me and being open during our conversations. Together with Lienke and Pauline, we went on quite a roller coaster but a highly enjoyable one at that. I had the privilege of experiencing your determination to bring out the best in people, and I sincerely value our collaboration.

The passion, support and expertise of the Mijnals Commission and my colleagues at Turner were truly heartwarming.

Katrien, Quilla, Yannick and Malú: I am grateful for your support, patience and the pride you shared with me.

PICTURE CREDITS

Page 1 (top right): Chris Turvey/PA Images/Alamy Stock Photo

Page 1 (bottom): Soccrates Images

Page 2 (top): Soccrates Images

Page 2 (bottom): Eric Verhoeven/Soccrates/Getty Images

Page 3 (top): Robin Utrecht /ABACAPRESS.COM/ABACA/PA Images/ Alamy Stock Photo

Page 3 (bottom): Olaf Kraak/EPA/Shutterstock

Page 4 (top): PA Images/Alamy Stock Photo

Page 4 (bottom): Mao Siqian/Xinhua/Alamy Live News

Page 5 (top left): Orange Pics BV/Alamy Live News

Page 5 (top right): Olaf Kraak/Hollandse Hoogte/Shutterstock

Page 5 (bottom): Lynne Cameron – The FA/The FA via Getty Images

Page 6 (top): Kieran Galvin/DeFodi Images via Getty Images

Page 6 (bottom left): Sportimage/Alamy Live News

Page 6 (bottom right): BBC Motion Gallery/Getty Images

Page 7 (top left): Charlotte Wilson/Offside/Offside via Getty Images

Page 7 (top right): Justin Tallis/AFP/Getty Images

Page 7 (bottom): Daniela Porcelli/SPP/Shutterstock

Page 8 (top): Quinn Rooney/Getty Images

Page 8 (bottom left): Norvik Alaverdian/NurPhoto via Getty Images

Page 8 (bottom right): Naomi Baker/The FA/The FA via Getty Images